Iona Community

HeAVeN ShALL NoT Wait

by

JOHN BELL & GRAHAM MAULE

with
The Wild Goose Worship Group

songs

VOLUME 1
Songs of Creation, the
Incarnation, and the Life
of Jesus

First Published 1987
Revised 1989

Dedicated

to

THE IONA COMMUNITY

with

love and gratitude

on its

Fiftieth Birthday

The Wild Goose is a Celtic symbol of the Holy Spirit.
It serves as the logo of Iona Community Publications.

Wild Goose Publications

The Publishing Division of the Iona Community
Pearce Institute, 840 Govan Road, Glasgow G51 3UT
Tel: 041 − 445 4561

Printed in Great Britain by
BPCC Paulton Books Limited

CONTENTS

A – GOD, CARING AND CREATING

B – GOD, COMING AMONG US

C – JESUS, ONE OF US

D – CHANTS AND RESPONSES

AN INTRODUCTION TO WILD GOOSE SONGS

(The Wild Goose is one of the Celtic symbols for the Holy Spirit)

We began singing and writing new songs not primarily because we were fed up with the old ones, but because others were and because we recognise that, in every era, Jesus looks for new bottles to hold his new wine.

This is not to discount the 'classical hymns of the church'. Indeed if we are not familiar with the great hymns which have shaped Christian life and faith through the centuries, we have little by which to judge modern writing.

The trouble is that not every old hymn is a great hymn. Many were ideally suited to their day, but that day has now gone. And in any case, does not God demand, through his servant psalm-writer, that we 'sing a **new** song to the Lord?' The church always needs new songs, not because the Gospel changes, but because the world changes and God's purposes in the world have to be re-interpreted to become real for the times; God's praise has to be sung in terms which are relevant rather than respectable but dated; and that which causes God's people to shout for joy or to suffer must be given expression which is contemporary with their experience.

Living in Scotland has sharpened our awareness of these needs.

We live in a country where unemployment plagues and demoralises large sections of our community, and where lochs play host to a nuclear arsenal which, if activated, could absolve nations and people from the next thousand years of existence. But where are the hymns of protest, the songs which carry the despair of dispossessed people and the anxiety of those who do not want to see the earth polluted and human life obliterated, courtesy of our neighbourhood armoury?

We live in a country which has a glorious heritage of folk music, of fiddle and pipe tunes, of vocal melodies all in danger of disappearing into oblivion. But where are the spiritual songs which have clothed themselves in this musical richness? Why is it that Africans, Asians and Central Americans have allowed the Gospel to take root in their folk music, but we in Britain have, by and large, avoided such an association as if Christ had never joyed to see children piping and dancing in the street?

We live in a country which, as elsewhere in the West, has witnessed a continuous decline in levels of church attendance yet, ironically, the majority of people claim to believe in God and accept the fact of Christ.

But where are the words and music which might yet allow those on the fringes of the church, or those who have rejected the trappings of organised religion, to deepen their faith and praise their maker?

We live in a country which, by virtue of its Celtic influences and history, had at the core of early Christian evangelising the affirmation that in Jesus, God took on matter, became part of the world, lit up the ordinary with holiness and did not despise the secular which he came to save. But where are the liturgies which allow the sacred to touch and transform the whole fabric of society rather than just the religious bits?

The Celts, like the ancient Jews, are our spiritual ancestors. Both, in different ways, recognised that the Spirit of God was not a docile holy plaything. The Jewish psalmist wrote of how, when everything seemed proper, it was God's will to 'shake my mountain refuge.' The Celtic monks, knowing that same restlessness and provocation which issues from the Almighty, depicted the Holy Spirit both as a dove **and** a wild goose. But where in our contemporary devotions are there glimpses that God, in the twentieth century, can be expected to surprise, contradict, upset or rile us in order that the kingdom may come?

The songs in this and the ensuing volumes try to correct these imbalances. They are, however, not **the** answer to the worship needs of the church. Only God has the answers, but we dare to believe that when we take their joy and frustration with worship to God, he may give to us some clues as to the way forward.

Thus, if there is any worth in these songs, it is not because they are the product of a gifted soul or fertile imagination working in solitude. They are, rather, the product of ongoing arguement, experiment, study, discussion, questioning and listening to the conversation of ordinary people. They are also the product of being stunned by the unquestionable relevance of the Word of God, which eyes, blinded by bias, presumption or cynicism, had long avoided.

Sometimes people ask how we write the songs. Here is a brief synopsis of the process:

> Someone has an insight or an idea which excites others and informs or challenges faith;
> John picks over it and drafts a rough copy of a song;
> Graham scrutinises, corrects and amends it;
> Somehow a tune emerges from a folk tradition or mid air;
> The tune is either left alone, given an accompaniement or harmonised;
> The Worship Group sing it through and comment on it;
> The song, now in its third version, is sung at public worship;
> A final revision is made.

Most songs in this collection followed that process. Some, like *The Faces of God*, started life in a bible study; others, like *Love and Anger*, came from listening to friends from the Third World; others yet, like 'God's Table, were written because there were no songs which celebrated the feeding of the 5000

In the main, the songs in the first two volumes, are about God, Jesus and the Holy Spirit. Several of them tell or comment on biblical stories. This is necessary in an age where fewer and fewer people can be assumed to know the scriptures. There are also a number of songs which express the delight or the apprehension of followers of Jesus, then and now. This too is necessary, for if our relationship with God is to be honest, it has to avoid platitudes and phrases which we think God might like to hear in preference to what we need to say. The third volume will concentrate more on the ceremonies of life and faith.

Most of the tunes in the book can be sung unaccompanied. This is a much forgotten traditional Scottish practise. Until the 1880's, most people suspected accompanied singing in worship: now many churches see an organist or pianist as an absolute necessity. But our common denominator is not manual dexterity, it is the ability to sing. If we learn new songs with voice alone, then the addition of a piano or other instrument is a bonus, not a prerequisite.

We do not suggest that the songs in this book be used in place of the traditional hymns of the church, they should be used as alternatives. And they should be used in conjunction with other 'alternatives' which come from other communities or musical traditions – Taize and Mission Praise being two.

In publishing these songs, we express our indebtedness to a wide range of known and unnamed people. Without the patience of our secretarial staff or the perseverance of our publisher; without the encouragement of the Iona Community, and particularly the resident group at the Abbey; without the trial and comment of individuals and congregations who told us what worked and what didn't; without the arguement and insight, the pain and joy of friends inside and outside the Church; and without the erratic and demanding provocation of the Wild Goose, the Holy Spirit of Almighty God, these songs would not be.

We hope you enjoy using this book. We hope that the words will, to a satisfactory extent, reflect your own experience of believing in the present tense. We hope that you will try the songs whose tunes you don't know, as well as those you instantly recognise.

But if it does not help to enrich your own and your church's worship, then pass the book to someone else and try something different. God's worship, as God's Church, is tartan in texture. This is only one thread.

John L. Bell
Graham A. Maule
September 1987

Please note: In this revised edition there are guitar chords given with some
               songs. These do **not** always correspond to harmony settings.

GOD, CARING AND CREATING

I AM FOR YOU

Tune: INCARNATION (JLB)

gently

Be - fore the world be-gan one Word was there; ____

ground-ed in God he was, root-ed in care; ____

by him all things were made, in him was love dis-played; ―

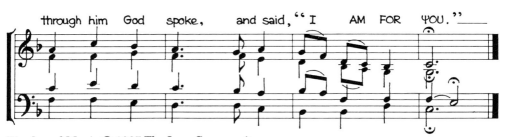

through him God spoke, and said, " I AM FOR YOU."____

1. Before the world began,
   One Word was there;
   Grounded in God he was,
   Rooted in care;
   By him all things were made,
   In him was love displayed;
   Through him God spoke, and said,
   "I AM FOR YOU".

2. Life found in him its source,
   Death found its end;
   Light found in him its course,
   Darkness its friend.
   For neither death nor doubt
   Nor darkness can put out
   The glow of God, the shout,
   "I AM FOR YOU".

3. The Word was in the world
   Which from him came;
   Unrecognised he was,
   Unknown by name;
   One with all humankind,
   With the unloved aligned,
   Convincing sight and mind,
   "I AM FOR YOU".

4. All who received the Word
   By God were blessed;
   Sisters and brothers they
   Of earth's fond guest.
   So did the Word of Grace
   Proclaim in time and space
   And with a human face,
   "I AM FOR YOU".

The Prologue to St. John's Gospel, of which this song is a paraphrase, celebrates that the world is not an accident. Its creation was and is rooted in the will and Word of God.

WE MET YOU

Tune: SEVEN DAYS (JLB)

with a steady beat

We met you, God, on Mon-day when you made the light and

Cm   Fm6/D   Cm/Eb   Fm6/D   G7   Cm

called the bright-ness day time and the dark — ness night.   We

Cm   Fm6/D   Cm/Eb   Fm   G7   Cm   Bb7

stum-bled when the light grew dim and floun-dered through the day and

Eb   Cm   Bb   Bb7   Db   Bbm7   Ab   G7

al — most missed the voice which called, "I AM THE WAY".   Fine.

Cm   Fm6/D   Cm/Eb   Fm6/D   G   C

Words and Music © 1987 The Iona Community

1. We met you, God, on Monday when you made the light
   And called the brightness daytime and the darkness night.
   We stumbled when the light grew dim and floundered through the day
   And almost missed the voice which called,
   "I AM THE WAY".

2. We met you, God, on Tuesday graced by sea and sky,
   In mystery unfathomed and delight so high.
   The poles of pain and passion we discovered in our youth
   And almost missed the voice which called,
   "I AM THE TRUTH".

3. We met you, God, on Wednesday when the land gave birth
   To fruit and flower and grain and grass all sprung from earth.
   We misused nature's kindness, turned beauty into strife
   And almost missed the voice which called,
   "I AM THE LIFE".

4. We met you, God, on Thursday in the stars and sun,
   Where skill and will and science found a race to run.
   We built our space invaders to threaten all we knew
   And almost missed the voice which called,
   "I'VE CHOSEN YOU".

5. We met you, God, on Friday making creatures move,
   Declaring birds and beasts and fish are gifts of love.
   We heard the tale of sheep and goats, the lamb hung on the tree
   And almost missed the voice which called,
   "COME, FOLLOW ME".

6. We met you, God, on Saturday when, in your mold,
   Both men and women walked and worked, grew wise and old.
   We thought your image good enough to engineer its end
   And almost missed the voice which called,
   "YOU ARE MY FRIEND".

7. We meet you, God, on Sunday when you take a rest
   As we attempt to hide our worst and show our best.
   We fail and wonder what to do till, faced with bread and wine,
   We hear the words, "THESE ARE FOR YOU
   AND YOU ARE MINE".

A series of slides from everyday life may be devised to illustrate this song.

THE GOODNESS OF GOD

Tune: GOODNESS (JLB)

Words and Music © 1987 The Iona Community

1. The goodness of God is the source of our gladness,
   Surrounding the world with a harness of care,
   Enabling surprise and allowing for sadness,
   The hope of recovery, present as air.

2. The life of the world is a heavenly treasure,
   A pleasure to ponder, a summons to move,
   A radical bias of God in creation
   Assuring the small and weakest of love.

3. The song of the earth has an infinite chorus,
   Resounding from birth through the silence of death,
   Expressive of anguish, frustration and laughter,
   It praises the Lord of music and breath.

4. The gifts of the poor are the means of our mending,
   As, touching their need, we are healed by their pain:
   The almost forgotten are meant by the Maker
   To challenge the rich to forfeit their gain.

5. In Jesus the goodness of God was incarnate,
   The life of the world was redeemed and restored,
   The song of the earth found the key to its meaning,
   The gifts of the poor were never ignored.

6. And Jesus is present in word and in Spirit
   Where all that is greatest belongs to the least,
   Where sign matches song in complete correspondence
   And those who were low sit high at the feast.

With a song of six verses like this one, it will be more enjoyable if
everyone sings only verse 3 and verse 6. Solo voices or one gender at a
time can do the others.

SHAKE UP THE MORNING

Tune: SHAKE UP (JLB)

Words and Music © 1987 The Iona Community

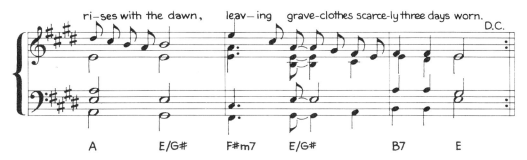

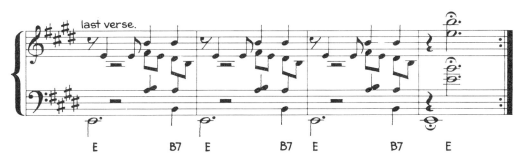

1. Shake up the morning, let the dawn undress,
   Let dew reglisten nature's loveliness;
   Waken the songbird and unseal the throat
   That greets the daybreak with a crystal note.
           Praise to the Lord, whose morning we inherit;
           Praise creation's fuse, the Holy Spirit;
           Praise to the Son who rises with the dawn,
           Leaving graveclothes scarcely three days worn.

2. Shake up the world and let the Kingdom come,
   The dumb be listened to, the lost find home;
   Make earthly politics the stuff of prayer
   Till want and warring are dispelled by care.
           Praise to the Lord whose world we inherit;
           Praise God's catalyst, the Holy Spirit;
           Praise to the Son whose choice it is to bless
           Those who work for peace and live on less.

3. Shake up the Church and let all Christians show
    That faith is real, that God is good to know;
    Fashion new symbols of the coming age
    When hope and love will take the centre stage.
    　　　Praise to the Lord whose Gospel we inherit;
    　　　Praise God's bird of love, the Holy Spirit;
    　　　Praise to the Son whose will and words decree
    　　　All are one in his community.

4. Shake up the evening, let the shadows range
    As clouds to castles in the sunset change;
    Kindle the moon and stars which through each night
    Reflect the glory of tomorrow's light.
    　　　Praise to the Lord whose evening we inherit;
    　　　Praise God's presence in the Holy Spirit;
    　　　Praise to the Son whose brightness none can kill,
    　　　Lighting paths for those who seek his will.

This accompanied song was written for a 'Feisd' — an international
youth event which takes place on Iona. It can be sung equally well in
the morning and evening.

DANCE AND SING

Tune: PULLING BRACKEN (Scottish Trad.)

DANCE AND SING, ALL THE EARTH, GRA-CIOUS IS THE HAND THAT TENDS YOU:
LOVE AND CARE EVE-RY-WHERE, GOD ON PUR-POSE SENDS YOU.

Shoot-ing star and sun-set shape the dra — ma of cre — a — tion;

light-ning flash and moon-beam share a com-mon der-i-va — tion.

Chorus: DANCE AND SING, ALL THE EARTH,
GRACIOUS IS THE HAND THAT TENDS YOU:
LOVE AND CARE EVERYWHERE,
GOD ON PURPOSE SENDS YOU.

1. Shooting star and sunset shape
   The drama of creation;
   Lightning flash and moonbeam share
   A common derivation.

2. Deserts stretch and torrents roar
   In contrast and confusion;
   Treetops shake and mountains soar
   And nothing is illusion.

3. All that flies and swims and crawls
   Displays an animation
   None can emulate or change
   For each has its own station.

4. Brother man and sister woman,
   Born of dust and passion,
   Praise the one who calls you friends
   And makes you in his fashion.

5. Kiss of life and touch of death
   Suggest our imperfection:
   Crib and womb and cross and tomb
   Cry out for resurrection.

Sing this song unaccompanied. Dance it to the sound of others singing.
It is set to a traditional Scottish tune and follows the course of creation
as celebrated in Genesis Ch. 1.

THE SONG

Tune: THE SONG (JLB)

brightly

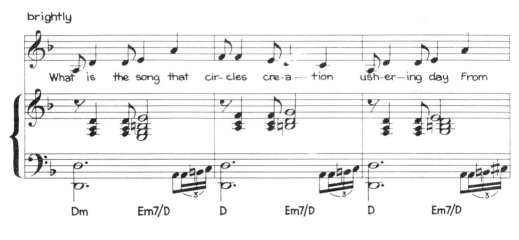

What is the song that cir‐cles cre‐a‐‐‐tion ush‐er‐ing day from

Dm   Em7/D   D   Em7/D   D   Em7/D

night?_____ What is the song that brings from the past the

D   F   Gm7/F   F   Gm7/F

hope of a fut—ure that's bright? THE SONG IS LOVE, GREAT‐ER THAN

F   Gm7/F   A   Em7   F/C

PLEA-SURE; THE SONG IS PLEA-SURE, GREAT-ER THAN PAIN; THE SONG IS

Dm7   G/D   B♭maj7   A

PAIN   THAT FINDS AN END-ING   AS LIFE BE-GINS WHERE DEATH HAS ONCE

Dm7   Em7/D   Dm   G/D   Gm7   Am7

D.C. last time.

LAIN.

last time.

Dm   Am7   Dm   Am7   D

1. What is the song that circles creation,
    Ushering day from night?
    What is the song that brings from the past
    The hope of a future that's bright?

Chorus: THE SONG IS LOVE, GREATER THAN PLEASURE;
    THE SONG IS PLEASURE, GREATER THAN PAIN;
    THE SONG IS PAIN THAT FINDS AN ENDING
    AS LIFE BEGINS WHERE DEATH HAS ONCE LAIN.

2. What is the song that promises freedom
    Where liberation's a dream?
    What is the song that says, with conviction,
    People are more than they seem.

3. What is the song that speaks of recovery
    When hope is ebbing away?
    What is the song that leads to discovery,
    Bringing new insights each day?

4. What is the song that tells how tomorrow
    Can be both different and great?
    What is the song that drowns the refrain
    That life is the servant of fate?

A lively accompaniment and solo verses enable this song be used to best effect.

WORLD WITHOUT END

Tune: BONNIE GEORGE CAMPBELL (Scottish Trad)

with a stately rhythm

Praise to the Lord for the joys of the earth :_____

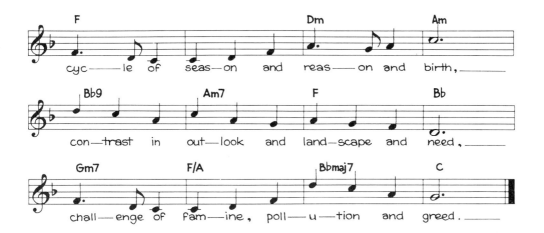

cyc——le of seas—on and reas——on and birth,____

con—trast in out—look and land—scape and need,____

chall——enge of fam——ine, poll——u—tion and greed.____

1. Praise to the Lord for the joys of the earth:
    Cycles of season and reason and birth,
    Contrasts in outlook and landscape and need,
    Challenge of famine, pollution and greed.

2. Praise to the Lord for the progress of life:
    Cradle and grave, bond of husband and wife,
    Pain of youth growing and wrinkling of age,
    Questions in step with experience and stage.

3. Praise to the Lord for his care of our kind:
    Faith for the faithless and sight for the blind,
    Healing, acceptance, disturbance and change,
    All the emotions through which our lives range.

4. Praise to the Lord for the people we meet,
    Safe in our homes or at risk in the street:
    Kiss of a lover and friendship's embrace,
    Smile of a stranger and words full of grace.

5. Praise to the Lord for the carpenter's son,
    Dovetailing worship and work into one:
    Tradesman and teacher and vagrant and friend,
    Source of all life in this world without end.

If an alternative melody is required, try *Slane*, an equally beautiful Irish melody, best known as the tune to *Be Thou My Vision*.

A WOMAN'S CARE

Tune: DIED FOR LOVE (English Trad.)

gently

When trou — ble strikes and fear takes root, and

dreams are dry and sense un — sound; when hope be — comes a

bar — ren waste, then doubts like mount — ains soar a — round.

1.   When trouble strikes and fear takes root,
     And dreams are dry and sense unsound;
     When hope becomes a barren waste,
     Then doubts like mountains soar around.

2.   Our wandering minds believe the worst
     And ask, as faith and fervour fade,
     "Has God now turned his back on us
       Forsaking those he loved and made?"

3.   God says, "See how a woman cares.
       Can she forget the child she bore?
       Even if she did, I shan't forget:
       Though feeling lost, I love you more."

4.   "My dearest daughter, fondest son,
       My weary folk in every land,
       Your souls are cradled in my heart,
       Your names are written on my hand."

5.   Then praise the Lord through faith and fear,
     In holy and in hopeless place;
     For height and depth and heaven and hell
     Can't keep us far from his embrace.

In Isaiah Ch. 49 divine love is likened to that of a woman.
Appropriately this paraphrase is set to the tune of another woman's
song – *Died For Love*. As an alternative, the tune *Rockingham* may
be used.

THE FACES OF GOD

Tune: HERE'S TO THE MAIDEN (English Trad.)

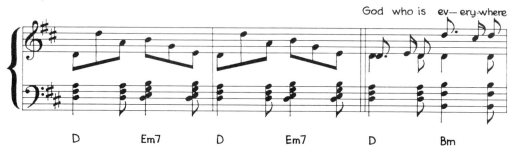

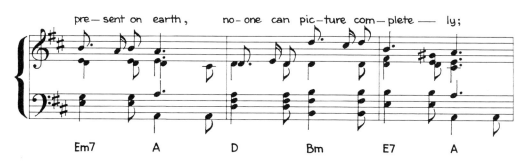

1.   God who is everywhere present on earth,
   No one can picture completely;
   Yet to the eye of the faithful he comes
   And shows himself always uniquely.

Chorus: SINGING OR SAD,
   WEEPING OR GLAD –
   SUCH ARE THE GLIMPSES OF GOD THAT WE'RE GIVEN.
   LAUGHTER AND CHEERS,
   ANGER AND TEARS –
   THESE WE INHERIT FROM EARTH AND FROM HEAVEN.

2.   Shrouded in smoke or else high on the hill,
   Quaking with nature's own violence –
   Thus was the Lord found, frightening his folk,
   But later he met them in silence.

3.   God is the father who teaches his child
   Wisdom and values to cherish;
   God is the mother who watches her young
   And never will let her child perish.

4.   Spear in the hand or with tears on the cheek,
   Monarch and shepherd and lover:
   Many the faces that God calls his own
   And many we've yet to discover.

5. Can we be certain of how the Lord looks,
    Deep though our faith and conviction,
    When in the face of the Saviour we see
    The smile of divine contradiction?

Throughout the bible, God is concerned that we see not just one side of
him, but all sides. This song, set to an English maypole tune explores
some of these sides or pictures.

PRAISE WITH JOY

Tune: PRAISE MY SOUL (J.Goss)

moderato

Praise with joy the world's Cre — a — tor, God of just—ice,
love and peace, source and end of hu — man know—ledge,
force of great-ness with—out cease. Cel — e — brate the
Ma — ker's glo — ry - power to res — cue and re — lease.

Words © 1987 The Iona Community

1. Praise with joy the world's Creator,
   God of justice, love and peace,
   Source and end of human knowledge,
   Force of greatness without cease.
   Celebrate the Maker's glory –
   Power to rescue and release.

2. Praise the Son who feeds the hungry,
   Frees the captive, finds the lost,
   Heals the sick, upsets religion,
   Fearless both of fate and cost.
   Celebrate Christ's constant presence –
   Friend and Stranger, Guest and Host.

3. Praise the Spirit sent among us,
   Liberating truth from pride,
   Forging bonds where race or gender,
   Age or nation dare divide.
   Celebrate the Spirit's treasure –
   Foolishness none dare deride.

4. Praise the Maker, Son and Spirit,
   One God in community,
   Calling Christians to embody
   Oneness and diversity.
   Thus the world shall yet believe, when
   Shown Christ's vibrant unity.

Written for the World Student Christian Federation's anniversary gathering in Edinburgh, 1985, this song of the Holy Trinity is set to one of the best loved English hymn tunes.

HOW LONG, O LORD?

Tune: NEW THIRTEENTH (JLB)

slow and bluesy

How long, O Lord, will you quite for-get

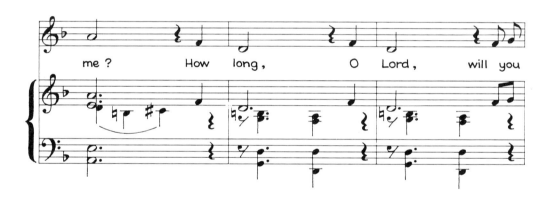

me?   How long, O Lord, will you

turn your face from me?   How long, O

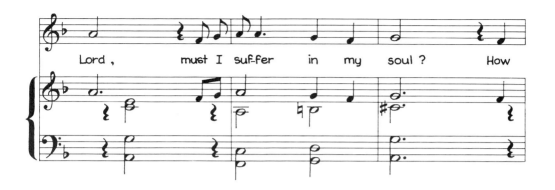

1. How long, O Lord,
   Will you quite forget me?
   How long, O Lord,
   Will you turn your face from me?
   How long, O Lord,
   Must I suffer in my soul?
   How long, how long,
   O Lord?

2. How long, O Lord,
   Must this grief possess my heart?
   How long, O Lord,
   Must I languish night and day?
   How long, O Lord,
   Shall my enemy oppress?
   How long, how long,
   O Lord?

3. Look now, look now
   And answer me, my God;
   Give light, give light,
   Lest I sleep the sleep of death.
   Lest my enemies
   Rejoice at my downfall,
   Look now, look now,
   O Lord.

Sometimes we have to call on God's care, because we have been made redundant, victimised, lost out in love or been hurt by people close to us. At such times the words of Psalm 13 can be very helpful.

THE SECRET

Tune: THE SECRET (JLB)

moderato

Pull back the veil on the dawn of cre—a—tion; van—ish the mists from the

Em   F#m   Em7   Bm7   Em   F#m

sourc—es of time;   ech—o the bird that broods ov—er the wa—ters,

Em7   Bm7   Em   F#m7   Em7   Bm7

sing—ing the se—cret of grace in its prime.   Love's _____ the

Em   F#m   Am7   Bm7 E   E

se—cret! _____   Love's _____ the   se—cret! _____

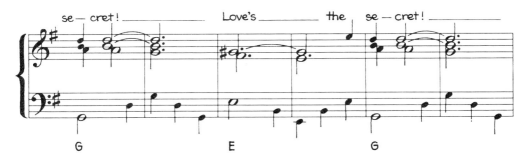

G   E   G

34

1. Pull back the veil on the dawn of creation;
    Vanish the mists from the sources of time;
    Echo the bird that broods over the waters,
    Singing the secret of grace in its prime.
            Love's the secret!
            Love's the secret!
        Love is God's risk and God's reason,
                God's rule and God's rhyme
                And God's rhyme.

2. Pull back the curtain on Bethlehem's stable;
    Strip off the tinsel and peer through the dark;
    Look at the child who's a threat yet in danger,
    Homeless and helpless he first makes his mark.
            Love's the secret!
            Love's the secret!
        Love is God's cradle, God's table,
                God's cup and God's ark,
                And God's ark.

3.   Pull back the veil on each parable's story,
Be it of virgins or talents forlorn;
Find in the kernel a core of compassion,
Planted in minds yet in flesh to be born.
          Love's the secret!
          Love's the secret!
          Love is God's madness, God's sadness,
               God's feast and God's corn,
               And God's corn.

4.   Pull back the curtain that hides what is holy;
Tear it in two as Christ did from the hill;
See at the centre of Good and bad Friday
Something no mob or marauder can kill.
          Love's the secret!
          Love's the secret!
          Love is God's way and God's witness,
               God's worth and God's will,
               And God's will.

5.   Pull back the stone that conceals what is buried;
Pull back the veil and the curtain of doom;
Pull back the centuries' doubts and delusions,
Look through the mystery into the tomb.
          Love's the secret!
          Love's the secret!
          Love is surprising, God's rising,
               God's wealth and God's womb,
               And God's womb.

This is definitely a piano rather than an organ tune. Each verse should be given a different volume, starting with the first verse quiet and mysterious.

GOD, COMING AMONG US

THE DAY OF THE LORD

Tune: AIR FALALALO (Scottish Trad.)

at a walking pace

The Day of the Lord shall come as proph—ets have told,_____ when Christ shall make all things new no mat-ter how old;_____ And some at the stars may gaze and some at God's word,_____ in vain to pre-dict the time the Day of the Lord._____ THE DES-ERT SHALL SPRING TO LIFE, THE HILLS SHALL RE-JOICE;_____ THE LAME OF THE EARTH SHALL LEAP, THE DUMB SHALL FIND VOICE;_____ THE LAMB WITH THE LION SHALL LIE, AND THE LAST SHALL BE FIRST;_____ AND NA-TIONS FOR WAR NO MORE SHALL STUD-Y OR THIRST._____

1. The Day of the Lord shall come
   As prophets have told,
   When Christ shall make all things new,
   No matter how old;
   And some at the stars may gaze,
   And some at God's word,
   In vain to predict the time,
   The Day of the Lord.

2. The Day of the Lord shall come:
   A thief in the night,
   A curse to those in the wrong
   Who think themselves right;
   A pleasure for those in pain
   Or with death at the door;
   A true liberation for
   The prisoners and poor.

3. The Day of the Lord shall come
   And judgement be known,
   As nations, like sheep and goats,
   Come close to the throne.
   Then Christ shall himself reveal
   Asking all to draw near,
   And see in his face all faces
   Once ignored here.

4. The Day of the Lord shall come,
   But now is the time
   To subvert earth's wisdom
   With Christ's folly sublime,
   By loving the loveless,
   Turning the tide and the cheek,
   By walking beneath the cross
   In step with the weak.

Chorus: THE DESERT SHALL SPRING TO LIFE,
THE HILLS SHALL REJOICE;
THE LAME OF THE EARTH SHALL LEAP,
THE DUMB SHALL FIND VOICE;
THE LAMB WITH THE LION SHALL LIE,
AND THE LAST SHALL BE FIRST;
AND NATIONS FOR WAR NO MORE
SHALL STUDY OR THIRST.

The sprightly walking tune needs no accompaniment, but the verses
may be sung by different groups or individuals.

THE WORD

Tune : VERBUM DEI (JLB)

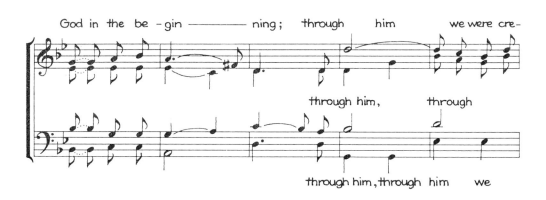

Words and Music © 1987 The Iona Community

1.   The Word was with God in the beginning,
    The Word was with God in the beginning;
    Through him we were created,
    <u>By him all</u> things <u>were made</u>.

2.   The Word was made known through the prophets,
    The Word was made known through the prophets;
    And though their speech was silenced
    <u>Still</u> their <u>witness went on</u>.

3.   The Word became flesh and lived among us,
    The Word became flesh and lived among us;
    And we beheld his glory,
    <u>Full of grace and truth</u>.

4.   Then praise the Word, softer than silence,
    And praise the Word, stronger than violence;
    Rejoice that in the body
    <u>Christ the Word is known</u> !

Essentially a choral rather than congregational song. The underlined words refer to the bass line.

THE CAROL OF GOD'S CHOICE

Tune: GARTHAMLOCK (JLB)

at a steady pace

No one would choose, to start a clan, a child—less coup-le late in years, _____ con-

F   C7   F   C7   F   Dm   Gm7   C

-tent to live in peace and quiet, past thought of trav-elling or car eers ; _____ till

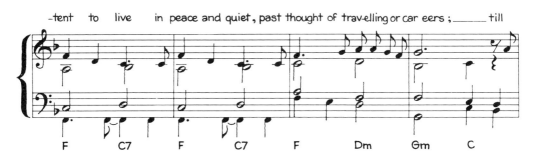

F   C7   F   C7   F   Dm   Gm   C

Ab-rah'm learned whom God was af-ter and Sa-rah's womb was filled with laugh—ter.

last verse only.

Am   Em   F   C/E   Dm   G7   C   C7   C

Words and Music © 1987 The Iona Community

1. No one would choose, to start a clan,
   A childless couple late in years,
   Content to live in peace and quiet,
   Past thought of travelling or careers;
   Till Abrah'm learned whom God was after
   And Sarah's womb was filled with laughter.

2. No one would choose, to free a tribe,
   A fugitive in shepherd' dress,
   Embarrassed by his stuttering tongue,
   Aware his past lay in a mess;
   Till Moses learned God's startling news
   That he should help to free the Jews.

3. No one would choose, to lead a race,
   A teenage boy who loved to sing,
   Unsuited to the sword or shield,
   Protected only by a sling;
   Till David helped God win the day
   And on the ground Goliath lay.

4. No one would choose, to save the world,
   A child of parents newly wed,
   Whom common folk received with joy
   And royal courts perceived with dread;
   Till God, in Jesus' infant voice,
   Confirmed the strangeness of his choice.

5. So let us join to bless this babe,
   The high, the humble and the low,
   The ones who think they've found their faith
   And those unsure of what they know.
   In wonder, welcome what God does —
   He loves and wants each one of us.

Let this song begin quietly, gradually increasing the number of sing-
ers until all join in verse 5.

GOD'S SURPRISE

Tune: SCARLET RIBBONS (English Trad.)

gently

Who would think that what was need-ed to trans-form and

G   Am   D7   G   C   Am6

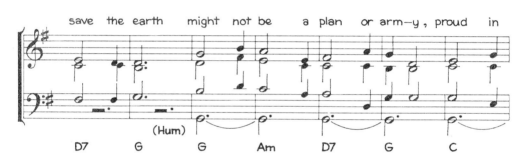

save the earth might not be a plan or arm-y, proud in

(Hum)

D7   G   G   Am   D7   G   C

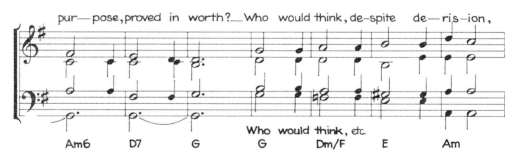

pur—pose, proved in worth?__Who would think, de-spite de—ris-ion,

Who would think, etc.

Am6   D7   G   G   Dm/F   E   Am

that a child should lead the way?___ God sur-pris——es

Am7   Bm7   Cmaj7   D7   G   Am

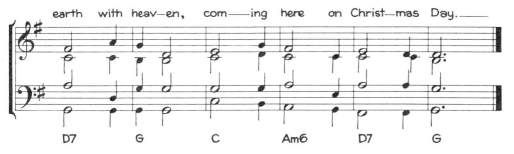

earth with heav—en, com——ing here on Christ—mas Day.____

D7   G   C   Am6   D7   G

1. Who would think that what was needed
    To transform and save the earth
    Might not be a plan or army,
    Proud in purpose, proved in worth?
    Who would think, despite derision,
    That a child should lead the way?
    God surprises earth with heaven,
    Coming here on Christmas Day.

2. Shepherds watch and wise men wonder,
    Monarchs scorn and angels sing;
    Such a place as none would reckon
    Hosts a holy helpless thing;
    Stable beasts and by-passed strangers
    Watch a baby laid in hay:
    God surprises earth with heaven
    Coming here on Christmas Day.

3. Centuries of skill and science
    Span the past from which we move,
    Yet experience questions whether,
    With such progress, we improve.
    While the human lot we ponder,
    Lest our hopes and humour fray,
    God surprises earth with heaven
    Coming here on Christmas Day.

Scarlet Ribbons is a beautiful melody. The harmonised setting is not difficult, and the song is especially effective when sung, in a darkened church, as midnight approaches on Christmas Eve.

THE CAROL OF THE NATIVITY

Tune: NATIVITY (JLB)

Words and Music © 1987 The Iona Community

48

1. A pregnant girl none will ignore:
    Her husband knocks a guest house door.
        Who is the girl?
        Why knock the door?
    Thus starts a tale of which there's more.

2. The door slams shut; they're left to find
    Cold comfort in a barn behind.
        Why slam the door?
        Why stay behind?
    "We're wanted out of sight and mind."

3. Some shepherds dance, some angels sing;
    Some child is born – no special thing.
        Why do you dance?
        Why do you sing?
    "To celebrate the birth of our King."

4. King Herod in his palace hears
    The news which rouses hate and fears.
        Why hate the news?
        Why rouse your fears?
    "No child shall take my place, my dears."

5. Three wise men watch and follow a star;
    They've journeyed long, they've come so far.
        Why do you watch?
        Why come so far?
    "To celebrate whose servants we are."

6. A child is born, a son is given:
    He sleeps on earth who rules in heaven.
        Who is this child?
        Where is this heaven?
    Both come alive where love is given.

To make this song a dialogue, get one group of people to sing lines 3 &
4 on their own with everyone singing the other lines. The rhythm
should be steady but lively.

HODIE

Tune: HODIE (JLB)

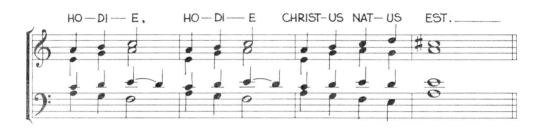

Words and Music © 1987 The Iona Community

Chorus: HODIE, HODIE
CHRISTUS NATUS EST.
HODIE, HODIE
CHRISTUS NATUS EST.

1. Gloria in excelsis;
    Pax in terra.
    Gloria in excelsis;
    Pax in terra.

2. Wanted and unwanted,
    Spoken and unsaid,
    Christ, the Word incarnate,
    Finds, near us, his bed.

3. Spotlights, crowds and fanfares
    Miss this tiny guest;
    Those who few would welcome
    At his birth are blessed.

4. Though he lives in danger,
    Cause of Herod's plight,
    Love surrounds the manger:
    Nothing shades his light.

5. Centuries thereafter
    Christ still comes again;
    Comes with threat and promise
    Now as much as then.

Hodie really needs to be sung either as a choral piece or with everyone singing the chorus and a group singing the verses in harmony.

THE AYE CAROL

Tune: AYE CAROL (JLB)

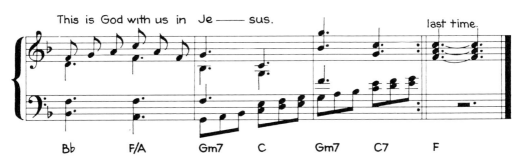

Words and Music © 1987 The Iona Community

1.   Who is the baby an hour or two old
      Looked for by shepherds far strayed from their fold,
      Lost in the world though more precious than gold?
      This is God with us in Jesus.

2.   Who is the woman with child at her breast,
      Giving her milk to earth's heavenly guest,
      Telling her mind to be calm and at rest?
      Mary, the mother of Jesus.

3.   Who is the man who looks on at the door,
      Welcoming strangers, some rich but most poor,
      Scanning the world as if somehow unsure?
      Joseph, the father of Jesus.

4.   Who are the people come in from the street,
      Some to bring presents and some just to meet,
      Joining their song to what angels repeat?
      These are the new friends of Jesus.

5.   Will you come with me, even though I feel shy,
      Come to his cradle and come to his cry,
      Give him your nod or your 'yes' or your 'aye',
      Give what you can give to Jesus?

It may be necessary in some parts of the world, to let people know that 'aye' means yes.

CLOTH FOR THE CRADLE

Tune: WAE'S ME FOR PRINCE CHARLIE (Scottish Trad.)

briskly

CLOTH FOR THE CRA – DLE, CRA-DLE FOR THE CHILD, THE CHILD FOR OUR EV-ER-Y JOY AND SOR — ROW;

G   Am7   D7   G   C   D

FIND HIM A SHAWL THAT'S WO-VEN BY US ALL TO WEL– COME THE LORD OF EACH TO-MOR—ROW.

G   Am7   D7   G   C   D

Dark-ness and light and all that's known by sight, sil— ence and ech—o fad — ing,

Am   G/B   D7   G   Am7   D7   G   D

weave in-to one a wel-come for the Son, set earth its own ma-ker ser-e-nad — ing. D.C.

Am   G/B   A7   D   G   Am7   D7

Words and Arrangement © 1987 The Iona Community

Chorus: CLOTH FOR THE CRADLE, CRADLE FOR THE CHILD,
THE CHILD FOR OUR EVERY JOY AND SORROW;
FIND HIM A SHAWL THAT'S WOVEN BY US ALL
TO WELCOME THE LORD OF EACH TOMORROW.

1.   Darkness and light and all that's known by sight,
Silence and echo fading,
Weave into one a welcome for the Son,
Set earth its own maker serenading.

2.   Claimant and queen, wage earners in between,
Trader and travelling preacher,
Weave into one a welcome for the Son,
Whose word brings new life to every creature.

3.   Hungry and poor, the sick and the unsure,
Wealthy, whose needs are stranger,
Weave into one a welcome for the Son,
Leave excess and want beneath the manger.

4.   Wrinkled or fair, carefree or full of care,
Searchers of all the ages,
Weave into one a welcome for the Son,
The Saviour of shepherds and of sages.

This song can easily be sung on its own, with a solo voice taking the verses. It can be used in a nativity setting, to allow everyone to walk forward and stand round the crib.

ONCE IN JUDAH'S
LEAST KNOWN CITY

Tune: IRBY (H.J.Gauntlett)

moderato

Once in Jud — ah's least known ci — ty stood a

board — ing house with back door shed, where an al — most sin-gle-par-ent

moth-er tried to find her new-born son a bed. ___ Ma — ry's

mum and dad went wild when they heard their daught-er had a child.

1. Once in Judah's least known city
   Stood a boarding house with back-door shed,
   Where an almost single-parent mother
   Tried to find her new-born son a bed.
   Mary's mum and dad went wild
   When they heard their daughter had a child.

2. He brought into earth a sense of heaven,
   Lord of none and yet the Lord of all;
   And his shelter always was unstable
   For his mission was beyond recall.
   With the poor, with those least holy,
   Christ the King was pleased to live so lowly.

3. Can he be our youth and childhood's pattern
   When we know not how he daily grew?
   Was he always little, weak and helpless,
   Did he share our joys and problems too?
   In our laughter, fun and madness,
   Does the Lord of love suspect our gladness?

4. Not in that uncharted stable
   With the village gossips standing by,
   But in heaven we shall see him —
   Here as much as up above the sky —
   If, in love for friend and stranger,
   We embrace the contents of the manger.

This is a song which knocks on the head some of the dubious assumptions surrounding Jesus' birth. So don't let it be sung too pompously. A harmonised version of the tune will be found in most hymnbooks.

DEO GRATIAS

Tune: DEO GRATIAS (JLB)

with a steady, sprightly rhythm

Had the Son of God been born in the place where kings are found,

we would have an eas-ier faith built on more at-trac-tive ground:

Je-sus jilt-ed hu-man fable by ap-pear-ing in a sta-ble.

first time only

De — o gra-ti-as, De — o gra-ti-as, De — o gra-ti — as.

De — o, De — o, De-o gra-ti — as.

1. Had the Son of God been born
    In the place where kings are found,
    We would have an easier faith
    Built on more attractive ground:
    Jesus jilted human fable
    By appearing in a stable.
    Deo Gratias, Deo Gratias,
    Deo Gratias.

2. Had the Son of God divorced
    Prayers from poverty and power,
    We would have an easier faith
    Vacuumed in a hallowed hour:
    Angels called for peace on earth
    Consequent to Jesus' birth.
    Deo Gratias, Deo Gratias,
    Deo Gratias.

3. Had the Son of God been met
    Without hindrance or alarm,
    We would have an easier faith
    Cossetted from those who harm:
    Herod, cruel and unimpressed,
    Made heaven's child forgo earth's rest.
    Deo Gratias, Deo Gratias,
    Deo Gratias.

4. Had the Son of God conformed
    To the pattern we would choose,
    All that leads to faith and love,
    Love would lack and faith would lose:
    God, undressed and laid in hay,
    Contradicts our will and way.
    Deo Gratias, Deo Gratias,
    Deo Gratias.

This is more of a choral piece and should be sung jauntily but clearly.

GOD BLESS US AND DISTURB US

Tune: GOD REST YOU MERRY (English Trad.)

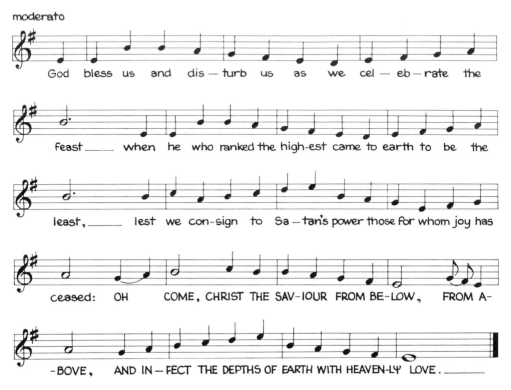

moderato

God bless us and dis—turb us as we cel—eb—rate the feast____ when he who ranked the high-est came to earth to be the least,____ lest we con-sign to Sa—tan's power those for whom joy has ceased: OH COME, CHRIST THE SAV-IOUR FROM BE-LOW, FROM A-BOVE, AND IN—FECT THE DEPTHS OF EARTH WITH HEAVEN-LY LOVE.____

1. God bless us and disturb us
   As we celebrate the feast,
   When he who ranked the highest
   Came to earth to be the least,
   Lest we consign to Satan's power
   Those for whom joy has ceased:

Chorus: O COME, CHRIST THE SAVIOUR
FROM BELOW, FROM ABOVE,
AND INFECT THE DEPTHS OF EARTH
WITH HEAVENLY LOVE.

2. Where Nicaragua's people
   Long for justice which is true;
   Where Ethiopia's children
   Cry for food which is their due;
   Where white South Africa declares
   Apartheid comes from you:

3. Where dealers thrive on heroin
   While junkies run from pain;
   Where mothers watch their addict sons
   Let life run down the drain;
   Where hope's a hit, a drink, a shot
   And death seems like a gain.

4. Where Christian folk detach themselves
   From following the cross
   By spotlighting the cradle
   As if that was all there was;
   Where who'll get what at Christmas
   Turns our minds from grace to dross:

5. To Bethlehem, Johannesberg,
   Whitehall and Possilpark;*
   To where a star is needed
   Since the dark is doubly dark;
   To where our lives await the Lord
   To set on us his mark:

Not so much a 'take-off' of a traditional choir, as an attempt to allow
the traditional Christmas spirit to spill over to where it is needed most.
*Possilpark is an area of Glasgow where drug addiction is rife. A more
appropriate name may be substituted and verses omitted as required.

SING A DIFFERENT SONG

Tune: DIFFERENT SONG (JLB)

vigorously

Sing a different song now Christmas is here ,

D   D   Em7/D   D

sing a song of peop-le know-ing God's near : The Mes-

A7   B

-si-ah is born in the face of our scorn , sing a differ-ent song to

Em7   A7   D   Gmaj7   D/F#   Bm   D/F#

wel-come and warn.

(last time)
Fine.

Em7   A7   D   D

1. Sing a different song now Christmas is here,
    Sing a song of people knowing God's near:
    The Messiah is born in the face of our scorn,
    Sing a different song to welcome and warn.

2. Shout a different shout now Christmas is here,
    Shout a shout of joy and genuine cheer:
    Fill the earth and sky with the news from on high,
    Shout a different shout that all may come by.

3. Love a different love now Christmas is here,
    Love without condition, love without leer:
    With the humble and poor, with the shy and unsure,
    Love a different love. Let Christ be the cure!

4. Dance a different dance now Christmas is here,
    Dance a dance of war on suffering and fear:
    Peace and justice are one and their prince is this Son.
    Dance a different dance. God's reign has begun!

Drums and tambourines can be used to let this lively carol dance.

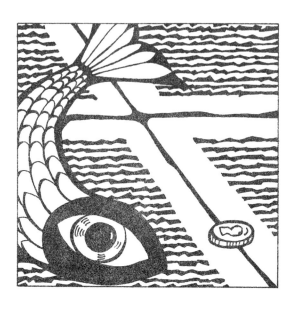

JESUS, ONE OF US

THE WORD OF LIFE

Tune: WILD MOUNTAIN THYME (Irish Trad.)

gently

In a byre near Beth——le—hem,_____ passed by man-y a

F   Bb/F   F   Bb

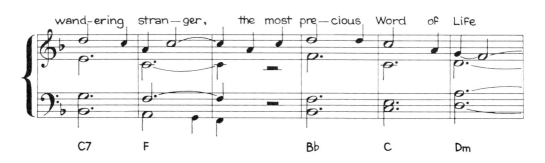

wand-ering stran—ger, the most pre—cious Word of Life

C7   F   Bb   C   Dm

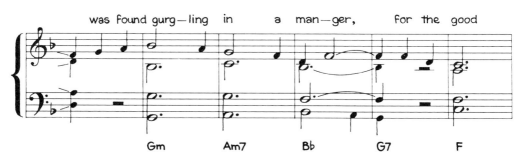

was found gurg—ling in a man—ger, for the good

Gm   Am7   Bb   G7   F

of us all._____ AND HE'S HERE WHEN WE CALL HIM,

Bb   F   Bb   C7   F

68

BRING—ING HEALTH, LOVE AND LAUGH—TER   TO LIFE NOW AND

Bb   C   Dm   Gm

EV——ER AF—TER,   FOR THE GOOD   OF US   ALL._____

Am7   Bb   Gm   F   Bb   F

1.   In a byre near Bethlehem,
        Passed by many a wand'ring stranger,
        The most precious Word of Life
        Was heard gurgling in a manger,
        For the good of us all.

Chorus: AND HE'S HERE WHEN WE CALL HIM,
        BRINGING HEALTH, LOVE AND LAUGHTER
        TO LIFE NOW AND EVER AFTER,
        FOR THE GOOD OF US ALL.

2.   By the Galilean Lake
        Where the people flocked for teaching,
        The most precious Word of Life
        Fed their mouths as well as preaching,
        For the good of us all.

3.   Quiet was Gethsemane,
        Camouflaging priest and soldier;
        The most precious Word of Life
        Took the world's weight on his shoulder,
        For the good of us all.

4.   On the hill of Calvary –
     Place to end all hope of living –
     The most precious Word of Life
     Breathed his last and died, forgiving,
     For the good of us all.

5.   In a garden, just at dawn,
     Near the grave of human violence,
     The most precious Word of Life
     Cleared his throat and ended silence,
     For the good of us all.

As with other songs of the Life of Christ, it may be useful to have a soloist sing the verses, with everyone responding. This traditionally happens with story-songs set to folk tunes.

GOD ON EARTH

Tune: O WALY WALY (English Trad.)

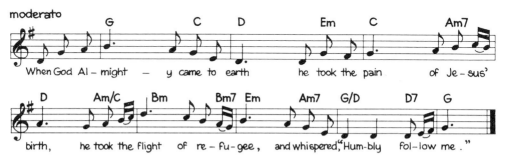

When God Al – might — y came to earth he took the pain of Je – sus'
birth, he took the flight of re – fu – gee, and whispered, "Hum-bly fol-low me."

1. When God Almighty came to earth
   He took the pain of Jesus' birth,
   He took the flight of refugee,
   And whispered, "Humbly follow me."

2. When God Almighty went to work,
   Carpenter's sweat he didn't shirk,
   Profit and loss he didn't flee,
   And whispered, "Humbly follow me."

3. When God Almighty walked the street,
   The critic's curse he had to meet,
   The cynic's smile he had to see,
   And whispered, "Humbly follow me."

4. When God Almighty met his folk,
   Of peace and truth he boldly spoke
   To set the slave and tyrant free,
   And whispered, "Humbly follow me."

5. When God Almighty took his place
   To save the sometimes human race,
   He took it boldly on a tree,
   And whispered, "Humbly follow me."

6. When God Almighty comes again,
   He'll meet us incognito as then;
   And though no words may voice his plea,
   He'll whisper, "Are you following me?"

Along with other songs in this section, *God on Earth* provides pictures from the life of Jesus. Such songs are often suitable for using with mime or slides illustrating the various stages in Jesus' ministry.

FOLLY AND LOVE

Tune: FOLLY AND LOVE (JLB)

sing _____ of a mo-ther and man — ger,
sing _____ of a fam-ily in dan — ger, _____

first time only.

crad-ling a threat and pre-par-ing a way; _____
Fath-er and Son and the Spir-it at play: _____

1. I sing of a mother and manger,
    Cradling a threat and preparing a way;
    I sing of a family in danger,
    Father and son and the spirit at play:
    Mother and babe,
    Father and son,
    Spirit and flesh
    And determined to stay.

2. I sing of a virgin and value,
    Lowest of low for the highest of high;
    I sing of a prince and a preview,
    Sinner and saint is he named and known by:
    Virgin and child,
    Lowest on high,
    Sinner and saint
    In response to earth's cry.

3. I sing of a woman and wedding,
    Marriage just passed and a bridegroom just born;
    I sing of new wine half encased in hay,
    Bread for the world first appearing as corn:
    Bridegroom and bride,
    Wine in the hay,
    Bread for the world
    Not yet broken or torn.

4. I sing of a wonder and wisdom,
    Maker of all all inspect or approve;
    I sing of an heir and a kingdom,
    Suckled and soon to be sought on the move:
    Wonder so wise,
    Maker on view,
    King in a crib,
    God is folly and love.

The first four lines are sung in unison; the last four, if possible, in two parts.

LORD, WHERE HAVE WE LEFT YOU?

Tune:—THE LICHTBOB'S LASSIE (Scottish Trad.)

gently
Lord, where have we left you — some where far a—way, re—mote and in the

man-ger, a stran-ger still in hay?_____ Lord, you ne-ver leave us._____
last time.

1. Lord, where have we left you —
   Somewhere far away,
   Remote and in the manger,
   A stranger, still in hay?

2. Lord, where have we left you —
   Somewhere lost to light,
   Submerged in doubt or dreaming
   And seeming out of sight?

3. Lord, where have we left you —
   Somewhere all can view,
   Well polished and presented,
   Undented and untrue?

4. Lord, where have we left you
   Somewhere out of range,
   Divorced from thoughts that matter,
   That shatter, cheat or change?

5. Lord, you never leave us,
   Though you're left behind.
   To where you call and need us,
   Now lead us and our kind.

   Lord, you never leave us.

It is both easy and effective to use this song, with its well-known tune,
as part of prayers of confession.

WHEN TO THE TEMPLE

Tune: THE HEMP DRESSER (Scottish Trad.)

not too quickly

When to the tem——ple, eight days young, Christ came for rit—ual bless——ing, he op—ened wide an old man's eyes and set his lips con—fess——ing, "This ba——by, cra—dled in my arms, shall suf—fer earth's of fenc——es. His life shall light the way to heaven and shat——ter smug pre—ten————ces."

Words © 1987 The Iona Community

1. When to the temple, eight days young,
   Christ came for ritual blessing,
   He opened wide an old man's eyes
   And set his lips confessing,
   "This baby, cradled in my arms,
      Shall suffer earth's offences.
      His life shall light the way to heaven
      And shatter smug pretences."

2. When in the temple, twelve years old,
   He sat among the sages,
   The questions flew, the insights dawned
   On folk of different ages.
   And to his parents, stunned to see
   Their son his faith defending,
   He said, "My father's work and will
      Are what I am attending."

3. When in the temple, later still,
   He saw unchecked extortion,
   With whip in hand and foot on stalls
   He scattered doves and fortune.
   "This House for Nations has become
      A sanctuary for thieving.
      Its founding purposes restore
      For prayer and for believing."

4. What shall we ask of Christ today
   In line with his intentions –
   To fill the Church with rage or prayer,
   Blessed babes or children's questions?
   Oh, let us pray for all of these
   And cease to be selective,
   For many are the means by which
   Christ makes his Church effective.

The tune suggested is originally a fiddle tune. It may therefore take a little while to match words and music. There are, however, several other folk or hymn tunes in the same metre, such as *The Vicar of Bray* (see Volume 3).

NAMES THEY CALLED HIM

Tune: THE BONNIE LASS O' FYVIE – O (Scottish Trad.)

at a walking pace

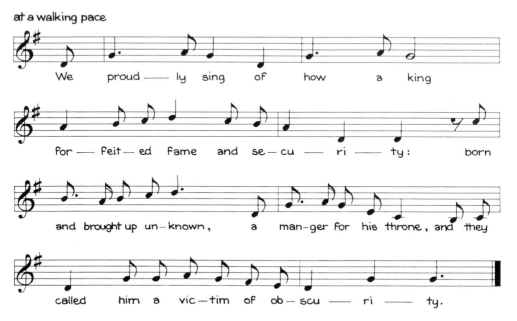

We proud — ly sing of how a king for — feit — ed fame and se — cu — ri — ty: born and brought up un — known, a man — ger for his throne, and they called him a vic — tim of ob — scu — ri — ty.

1.   We proudly sing
     Of how a king
     Forfeited fame and security:
     Born and brought up unknown,
     A manger for his throne,
     And they called him a victim of obscurity.

2.   In faith he grew,
     In wisdom too,
     Learning and loving with every breath;
     He served his time and trade,
     As furniture he made,
     And they called him the carpenter of Nazareth.

3.   Twelve friends he called
     Were soon involved
     Sharing his mission to shire and slum;
     He healed the sick and sad,
     He helped the poor and mad,
     And they called him the man who made the kingdom come.

4.   For doing good,
     For where he stood,
     Rumours were spread with the worst intent;
     His critics, unimpressed,
     Disparaged those he blessed,
     And they called him a threat to the establishment.

5.   Cruel and detatched,
     A plot they hatched,
     Leading to death on the gallows tree;
     Those who his grace had seen
     Refused to intervene,
     And they called him the dross of all humanity.

6.   And yet we sing –
     This is the king
     Who neither death nor deceit can kill.
     By rising to forgive,
     He sets us free to live
     And he calls us to be his friends and followers still.

       Ideally, a fife and drum should accompany this song.

THE TEMPTATIONS

Tune: FORTY DAYS (JLB)

moderato

For for—ty days and for—ty nights, the des—ert waste was
Jes—us' home. Bap—tised and blessed, God let him stay where
thoughts of fame and for—tune roam. If doubt is deep and
faith is small, the des—ert place is where he'll stall: if
faith is deep and doubt is thin, the des—ert place is where he'll win.

1.   For forty days and forty nights,
The desert place was Jesus' home.
Baptised and blessed, God let him stay
Where thoughts of fame and fortune roam.
If doubt is deep and faith is small,
The desert place is where he'll stall:
If faith is deep and doubt is thin,
The desert place is where he'll win.

2. In unknown parts, where strangers meet,
   To build a bridge, they sit and eat.
   But where there's neither drink nor food,
   What can be done to make things good?
   "Why not decline to be ill fed?
     Command these stones to turn to bread."
   "Why crave for bread, when God alone
     Fulfills more needs than transformed stone?"

3. Above the world's most holy place,
   The sight below cries out for grace:
   To jump down from the temple's tower
   Would show God's mercy and heaven's power.
   "If faith and love are more than charms,
     Let angels catch you in their arms."
   "Though angels come at my behest,
     I will not set the Lord a test."

4. A mountain top reveals the earth
   In all its tragedy and mirth;
   Nations and people need a king
   To wisely govern everything.
   "All that you want, and all you see,
     Is yours if you will worship me."
   "All that I see is God's to give,
     To him I pray, for him I live."

5. For forty days and forty nights
   The desert place was Jesus' home.
   Baptised and blessed, God let him stay
   Where thoughts of fame and fortune roam.
   And, we who follow Christ today,
   Are prone to hear the tempter's voice.
   And whether we say Yes or No
   Is our, not God's, peculiar choice.

The bare tune is evocative of the barren desert in which Jesus was tempted. The song involves a dialogue between Jesus and Satan. At such parts, it can be effective to use two different solo voices.

THE SON OF MARY

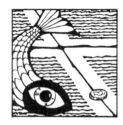

Tune: BUY BROOM BESOMS (Geordie Trad.)

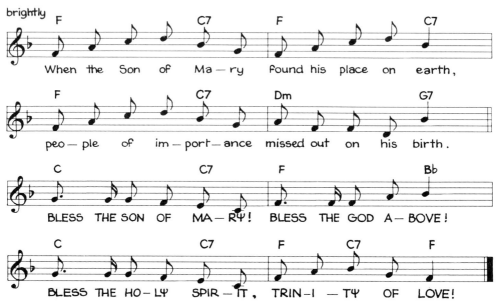

When the Son of Ma-ry found his place on earth,
peo-ple of im-port-ance missed out on his birth.
BLESS THE SON OF MA-RY! BLESS THE GOD A-BOVE!
BLESS THE HO-LY SPIR-IT, TRIN-I-TY OF LOVE!

A. CHRISTMAS VERSION

1. When the Son of Mary
   Found his place on earth,
   People of importance
   Missed out on his birth.

Chorus: BLESS THE SON OF MARY!
   BLESS THE GOD ABOVE!
   BLESS THE HOLY SPIRIT,
   TRINITY OF LOVE!

2. When the Son of Mary
   Wearied for his bed,
   Straw and wool were gathered
   Round the cattle shed.

3. When the Son of Mary
   Sucked his mother's breast,
   Joseph kept a lookout,
   Fearing Herod's quest.

4. When the Son of Mary
   Cried a baby's cry,
   Stable guests kept silent:
   God could yell and sigh!

5. When the Son of Mary
   Comes this Christmas morn,
   Make your heart the manger
   Where his love is born.

B. GENERAL VERSION

1. When the Son of Mary
   Walked beside the sea,
   Nets were needing mending,
   Folk were needing free.

Chorus: BLESS THE SON OF MARY !
   BLESS THE GOD ABOVE !
   BLESS THE HOLY SPIRIT,
   TRINITY OF LOVE !

2. When the Son of Mary
   Walked along the street,
   Health he brought to lepers,
   Cripples to their feet.

3. When the Son of Mary
   Walked across the square,
   Children turned to dancing,
   Adults turned to stare.

4. When the Son of Mary
   Walked up to the cross,
   God saw him as winner,
   Others saw his loss.

5. When the Son of Mary
   Walks the world today,
   It's our feet he uses
   When his words we say.

Sometimes when these songs are used with children, they make signs at the chorus: hands in the shape of a cross for the Son, pointing upwards for 'God above' and in the shape of a dove for the Spirit.

SING HEY FOR THE CARPENTER

Tune: SING HEY (JLB)

with spirit

Come with me, come wan-der, come wel-come the world where stran-gers might smile or where stones may be hurled; Come leave what you cling to, lay down what you clutch and find, with hands emp-ty, that hearts can hold much. SING HEY FOR THE CAR-PEN-TER LEAV-ING HIS TOOLS! SING HEY FOR THE PHAR-I-SEES LEAV-ING THEIR RULES! SING HEY FOR THE FISH-ER-MEN LEAV-ING THEIR NETS! SING HEY FOR THE PEOP-LE WHO LEAVE THEIR RE-GRETS!

1. Come with me, come wander, come welcome the world
    Where strangers might smile or where stones may be hurled;
    Come leave what you cling to, lay down what you clutch
    And find, with hands empty, that hearts can hold much.

Chorus: SING HEY FOR THE CARPENTER LEAVING HIS TOOLS!
        SING HEY FOR THE PHARISEES LEAVING THEIR RULES!
        SING HEY FOR THE FISHERMEN LEAVING THEIR NETS!
        SING HEY FOR THE PEOPLE WHO LEAVE THEIR REGRETS!

2. Come walk in my company, come sleep by my side,
    Come savour a lifestyle with nothing to hide;
    Come sit at my table and eat with my friends,
    Discovering that love which the world never ends.

3. Come share in my laughter, come close to my fears,
    Come find yourself washed with the kiss of my tears;
    Come stand close at hand while I suffer and die
    And find in three days how I never will lie.

4. Come leave your possessions, come share out your treasure,
    Come give and receive without method or measure;
    Come loose every bond that's resisting the Spirit,
    Enabling the earth to be yours to inherit.

As with many other tunes in the folk idiom, an accompaniment is a great disadvantage, either on piano or guitar. However a bodrhan or other drum-like instrument can be an advantage when used with the chorus.

HEY MY LOVE

Tune: LADY MAISRY (Scottish Trad.)

slowly & meditatively

Blessed are the ones I call the poor, hey my love and ho my joy; blessed are the ones I call the poor, who dear—ly love me;_____ blessed are the ones I call the poor, God shall their King—dom's place en—sure: HIS KING-DOM IS OF HEAV-EN, OF EARTH, OF FIRE, OF LOVE.___

1.   Blessed are the ones I call the poor,
       Hey my love and ho my joy;
       Blessed are the ones I call the poor
       Who dearly love me;
       Blessed are the ones I call the poor,
       God shall their kingdom's place ensure:
Chorus: HIS KINGDOM IS OF HEAVEN,
                       OF EARTH,
                       OF FIRE,
                       OF LOVE.

2.   Blessed are the ones who deeply mourn . . .
       God's comfort in their hearts is known . . .

3.   Blessed are the ones who know their need . . .
       In them God's promises take seed . . .

4.   Blessed are the ones who thirst for right . . .
       Their journey's end is filled with light . . .

5.   Blessed are the ones who pardon all . . .
       With equal grace they'll hear God's call . . .

6.   Blessed are the ones whose pure hearts shine . . .
       They'll see their Lord and with him dine . . .

7.   Blessed are the ones who work for peace . . .
       As God's own children they'll increase . . .

8.   Blessed are the ones the world puts down . . .
       They'll have the Kingdom for their own . . .

Sing this very gently as a meditation, selecting verses appropriate to
the occasion if preferred.

POWER

Tune: THE KEEL ROW (Geordie Trad.)

Power stalks the earth both by pur — pose and ac — ci-dent,

fill — ing with pride those it does not fill with fear.

Power may be hid — den or power may be ev — i-dent,

mac — ro or mic — ro far off or ver — y near.

Look to the one who has cho — sen to live with-out

power to se-duce or cor-rupt or to re-pel;

Learn from the one who re-fus — es to scream and shout,

yet can con-vince that with him all will be well.

Words © 1987 The Iona Community

88

1. Power stalks the earth both by purpose and accident,
    Filling with pride those it does not fill with fear.
    Power may be hidden or power may be evident,
    Macro or micro, far off or very near.
    Look to the one who has chosen to live without
    Power to seduce or corrupt or to repel;
    Learn from the one who refuses to scream and shout,
    Yet can convince that with him all will be well.

2. Power of computer to file information may
    Keep for the few what the many should be told.
    Power of the party which governs the nation can
    Seldom be challenged and rarely be cajoled.
    Look to the one who embraces the frightened folk,
    Those more aware of the wrong than of their right;
    Learn from the one who will speak for the silenced ones,
    Hear for the deaf, and provide the blind with sight.

3. Power of the privileged in talent or parentage
    Discounts whoever it cannot understand.
    Power of the bureaucrat, anxious at every stage,
    Struggles to keep what's unstructured close at hand.
    Look to the one who forgoes his advantages,
    Sits on the ground with whoever cannot stand;
    Learn from the one who has known our predicament,
    Baffled all systems, and lived from mouth to hand.

4. Power of the press on the button or media
    Kindles the fuse to a scandal or a bomb;
    Power of the keeper of secret or confidence
    Puzzles what purpose to use the secret for.
    Look to the one who speaks peace unpretentiously,
    Defuses hate and is antidote for fears;
    Learn from the one who accepts, unconditionally,
    Those whom he summons to share his joy and tears.

There's always the danger that this song will go too fast for people to put words to the music. This can be avoided by having males and females or two different groups alternate verses or, better still, half verses.

THE SONG OF THE CROWD

Tune: KINGSFOLD (English Trad.)

To him who walks a-mong the crowds let's show our gra-ti-tude: _____ we
came to him a hun-gry mob, and his re-sponse was food. _____ This
is the teach-er well re-nowned for talk of sin for-given. _____ Some
prize his smile, some pull his robe, some say he comes from heaven. _____

1. To him who walks among the crowds
   Let's show our gratitude:
   We came to him a hungry mob,
   And his response was food.
   This is the teacher well renowned
   For talk of sin forgiven.
   Some prize his smile, some pull his robe,
   Some say he comes from heaven.

2. Who are you, lean faced traveller
   Whose words surpass all law,
   Whose past was spent in industry
   With hammer, nails and saw?
   Who are you, time-served carpenter
   Now that you've changed your trade
   To hosting casual lakeside feasts
   With food you never made?

3. But why the silent modesty,
   And why the shaking head?
   You're worth a thousand bakers
   For you multiply the bread!
   We'll make you king and gladly sing
   Songs to re-tell your story.
   So why not stay? Why move away?
   Do you refuse our glory?

4. There goes the man whose eyes can scan
   A crowd and tell their need.
   There goes the one whose words we shun
   When keen to frown or feed.
   He walks from here while people peer
   At his all-knowing face
   Which speaks of how each one who stares
   Has, in his heart, a place.

This is a song about a particular event and should be sung only in relation to the story of the feeding of the 5000.

GOD'S TABLE

Tune: GOD'S TABLE (JLB)

lively

Since the world was young, there's a song that's been sung of a pro—mise com—ing

Dm   C   Bbmaj7   Am7

true: _____ hun-gry folk will eat and long lost friends will meet and the

D   Dm   C

Lord will make all things new. _____ GOD _____ HAS A

Bbmaj7   Am7   Dm   Bbmaj7

TA—BLE WHERE HE CALLS HIS FRIENDS TO A FEAST THAT NE-VER ENDS;

Am7   F   C   F   Gm7   Am7

GOD_____ HAS A TA-BLE   AND ONE DAY WE'LL MEET HIM

B♭maj7   Am7   B♭   Am7

THERE._____   except last time.   last time.

Dm   A7   Dm   A7   G   D

1. Since the world was young,
    There's a song that's been sung
    Of a promise coming true:
    Hungry folk will eat
    And long-lost friends will meet
    And the Lord will make all things new.

Chorus: GOD HAS A TABLE
    WHERE HE CALLS HIS FRIENDS
    TO A FEAST THAT NEVER ENDS;
    GOD HAS A TABLE
    AND ONE DAY WE'LL MEET HIM THERE.

2. Jesus saw a crowd
    Who were hungry, and vowed
    That they didn't have much food.
    So he fed that bunch
    With a little boy's lunch
    As a sign that God is good.

3. Jesus told a tale
    Of how rich people fail
    To accept God's summons to dine.
    Then before their eyes,
    Those without earthly ties
    Share heaven's finest food and wine.

4. Till we hear that word
    From the mouth of the Lord
    Saying "Join me at my table",
    For the world we'll care
    And its good things we will share
    As long as we are able.

An agape, a harvest thanksgiving or celebration of the sacrament may all be suitable for using this song.

GIFTS OF THE SPIRIT

Tune: PERSONENT HODIE (German Trad.)

firmly

When our Lord walked the earth, all the world found its worth;

Dm   Em7   Am7   Dm   G   Am

as de-clared at his birth, God be-came our neigh—bour,

G   Am   Em   F   C   Am7   Dm

grant-ing with his fav—our, POWER TO SPEAK AND HEAL, GRACE TO

C   Am   Dm   C   A7

KNOW WHAT'S REAL, WIS-DOM, IN-SIGHT AND FAITH, LOVE AND UN-DER-STAND-ING.

Dm   G9   Em   Dm   Em   Am7   Dm

1. When our Lord walked the earth,
   All the world found its worth;
   As declared at his birth,
   God became our neighbour,
   Granting, with his favour,

Chorus: POWER TO SPEAK AND HEAL,
   GRACE TO KNOW WHAT'S REAL,
   WISDOM, INSIGHT AND FAITH,
   LOVE AND UNDERSTANDING.

2. Through his life, through his death,
   Through each gesture and breath,
   Jesus joined faith and deed,
   Model for our caring,
   Showing and yet sharing

3. Jesus loves all his friends
   And that love never ends;
   To his Church gifts he sends
   Through the Holy Spirit.
   These we still inherit:

4. Sing and smile and rejoice,
   Clap your hands, raise your voice;
   For, with unnerving choice,
   God, in Christ, has found us
   And displays around us

Since this song ennumerates the gifts of the Holy Spirit, it can be appropriately used to celebrate Pentecost as well as the life of Jesus.

OH WHERE ARE YOU GOING?

Tune: LAREDO(American Trad.)

Words © 1987 The Iona Community

1. Oh where are you going,
    And can I come with you,
    And what is your method
    For keeping alive:
    No pack or possessions,
    No clothing or shelter,
    No food to sustain you –
    How can you survive?

2. Oh where are you going,
    And can I come with you,
    And why is your company
    Never the same?
    You sit among beggars,
    You argue with bankers,
    Debate with the lawyers
    And walk with the lame.

3. Oh where are you going,
    And can I come with you,
    And what can you show
    For your talents and time —
    No profit from trading,
    No thing of your making,
    No mark or momento,
    No picture or rhyme?

4. Oh where are you going,
    And can I come with you,
    And what is the secret
    Towards which you strive?
    What hidden inspirer,
    What unseen admirer,
    What dream is the substance
    Upon which you thrive?

5. I'm going on a journey
    And welcome companions,
    But don't ask me
    How we'll survive, where we'll go,
    Or who will come with us,
    Or what we'll be doing.
    Just join me in travelling
    And learn all I know.

If preferred, five people might share this song — four 'disciples' asking
the questions in verses 1 — 4 from different parts of the church or room
and the fifth, Jesus, answering.

I'LL LOVE THE LORD

Tune: MACDOWELL (JLB)

gently

I'll love the Lord with all that lies in—side me,— I'll love the

Lord with bo-dy, soul and mind.——— I'LL LOVE THE LORD WITH ALL THAT

LIES IN—SIDE ME,—— I'LL LOVE THE LORD WITH BO-DY, SOUL AND

MIND.——— And ev—ery good-ness, ev-ery bless-ing in the Lord I'll

Words and Music © 1987 The Iona Community

find. AND EV—ERY GOOD-NESS, EV—ERY BLESS-ING IN THE LORD I'LL

FIND. I'LL LOVE THE LORD WITH ALL THAT LIES IN——SIDE ME,

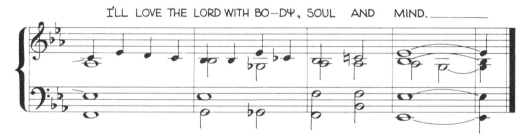

I'LL LOVE THE LORD WITH BO—DY, SOUL AND MIND.————

1.   I'll love the Lord with all that lies inside me,
     I'll love the Lord with body, soul and mind.

     Response: I'LL LOVE THE LORD WITH ALL THAT LIES INSIDE
                   ME,
                   I'LL LOVE THE LORD WITH BODY, SOUL AND
                   MIND.

     And every goodness, every blessing in the Lord I'll find.

     Response: AND EVERY GOODNESS, EVERY BLESSING IN THE
                   LORD I'LL FIND
                   I'LL LOVE THE LORD WITH ALL THAT LIES INSIDE
                   ME,
                   I'LL LOVE THE LORD WITH BODY, SOUL AND
                   MIND.

2.   I'll walk the path that Christ has walked before me,
     I'll give my yes to him who gave me all.   *(Response)*

     In every sound and every silence I will hear his call.   *(Response)*

3. I'll let my life be open to God's Spirit,
   To make me new and set my faith on fire. *(Response)*

   More than all things his peace and presence are what I desire. *(Response)*

4. I'll love the Lord with all that lies inside me,
   I'll love the Lord with body, soul and mind. *(Response)*

   And every goodness, every blessing in the Lord I'll find. *(Response)*

This is particularly effective when sung as a vesper at evening worship.

THE MIRACULOUS CATCH

Tune: SCARBOROUGH FAIR (Irish Trad.)

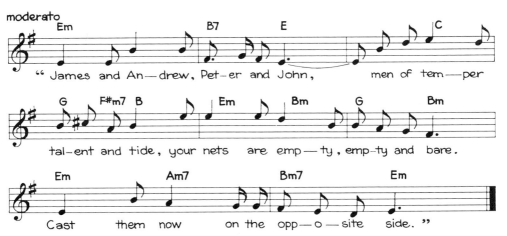

"James and An—drew, Pet—er and John, men of tem——per tal—ent and tide, your nets are emp—ty, emp—ty and bare. Cast them now on the opp—o—site side."

1. "James and Andrew, Peter and John,
    Men of temper, talent and tide,
    Your nets are empty, empty and bare.
    Cast them now on the opposite side."

2. "Jesus, you're only a carpenter's son:
    Joints and joists are part of your trade,
    But ours the skill to harvest the deep.
    Why presume to come to our aid?"

3. "Friends of mine and brothers through love,
    I mean more than fishing for food.
    I call your skill to service my will,
    Call your lives to harvest the good."

4. "Cast your nets where you think is right.
    Spend your lives where you think is need.
    But if you long for that which is best,
    Let it be on my word you feed."

5. "Stir then the waters, Lord, stir up the wind.
    Stir the hope that needs to be stretched.
    Stir up the love that needs to be ground,
    Stir the faith that needs to be fetched."

6. James and Andrew, Peter and John
    And the girls who walked by his side,
    Hear how the Lord calls each by their name
    Asking all to turn like the tide.

As with other songs referring to a particular occasion, the words may seem out of place if divorced from the biblical story they relate to. As suggested by the words, a solo voice, disciples voices and all others may, severally, share the verses.

HEAVEN SHALL NOT WAIT

Tune: HEAVEN SHALL NOT WAIT (JLB)

majestically

Heaven shall not wait for the poor to lose their pat — ience,

the scorned to smile, the des-pised to find a friend: _____

Je-sus is Lord, he has cham-pioned the un — want — ed;

in him in-just — ice con-fronts its time — ly end. _____

1. Heaven shall not wait
    For the poor to lose their patience,
    The scorned to smile, the despised to find a friend:
    Jesus is Lord;
    He has championed the unwanted;
    In him injustice confronts its timely end.

2. Heaven shall not wait
    For the rich to share their fortunes,
    The proud to fall, the elite to tend the least:
    Jesus is Lord;
    He has shown the masters' privilege –
    To kneel and wash servants' feet before they feast.

3. Heaven shall not wait
    For the dawn of great ideas,
    Thoughts of compassion divorced from cries of pain:
    Jesus is Lord;
    He has married word and action;
    His cross and company make his purpose plain.

4. Heaven shall not wait
    For our legalised obedience,
    Defined by statute, to strict conventions bound:
    Jesus is Lord;
    He has hallmarked true allegience –
    Goodness appears where his grace is sought and found.

5. Heaven shall not wait
    For triumphant Hallelujahs,
    When earth has passed and we reach another shore:
    Jesus is Lord
    In our present imperfection;
    His power and love are for now and then for evermore.

Note that the last line in the last verse is slightly longer than that of
other verses and the music changes to suit.

THE SAVIOUR

Tune: SAVIOUR (JLB)

quietly & slowly

Sitt-ing next to no-one, he makes mon-ey out of fools;_____

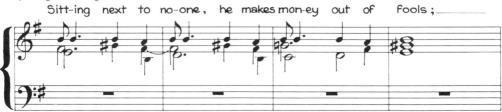

fak-ing scales of just-ice and re-writ-ing half the rules;_____

tired of mak-ing prof-it from the eas—y wage of sin;_____

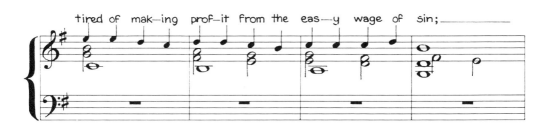

keen he is to stop, but where on earth can he be—gin? AND I

106

STILL KNOW I'LL KNOW, SHOULD WE NEV—ER MEET A—GAIN, WHAT YOUR

LOVE _____ MEANT _____ THEN. _____

Fine.

Words and Music © 1987 The Iona Community

1. *Cantor:* Sitting next to no one,
He makes money out of fools;
Faking scales of justice
And rewriting half the rules;
Tired of making profit
From the easy wage of sin;
Keen he is to stop,
But where on earth can he begin?

Voice: AND I STILL KNOW I'LL KNOW,
SHOULD WE NEVER MEET AGAIN,
WHAT YOUR LOVE MEANT THEN.

2. *Cantor:*   No one going near him,
                  Most folk turn and walk away;
                  Eaten by diseases,
                  He grows weaker every day;
                  Just a social leper,
                  Seeking someone in the street;
                  One of life's untouchables
                  Who no one wants to meet.

   Voice: AND I STILL KNOW I'LL KNOW,
                  SHOULD WE NEVER MEET AGAIN,
                  WHAT YOUR LOVE MEANT THEN.

3. *Cantor:*   A woman of convenience,
                  For the gentlemen of leisure;
                  A rag on whom they wipe themselves,
                  Pretending that it's pleasure.
                  Oh, how she shrinks
                  From the terror of their stare:
                  Those who tried to own her
                  Now would stone her, free of care.

   Voice: AND I STILL KNOW I'LL KNOW,
                  SHOULD WE NEVER MEET AGAIN,
                  WHAT YOUR LOVE MEANT THEN.

4.   *Cantor:*   Pockets full of money
                     And a head packed full of skill;
                     Proud beyond presumption,
                     Self assured and strong of will;
                     Craved for as an ally,
                     But unwanted as a friend;
                     The paragon of knowledge
                     Has a soul he hopes can mend.

     Voice: AND I STILL KNOW I'LL KNOW
                     SHOULD WE NEVER MEET AGAIN,
                     WHAT YOUR LOVE MEANT THEN.

5.   *Cantor:*   Teacher and disputer
                     And accepter of the lost;
                     Counsellor and Curer,
                     Never telling of the cost
                     Till one hellish Friday,
                     Silhouetted on a tree,
                     The one who heals creation
                     Took the pain imposed by me.

                     And I still know I'll know,
                     Should we never meet again
                     What your love meant then.

To use this song visually, have one person as cantor and four others who, one at a time, mime out their character, stopping to sing the relevant chorus in the first four verses.

WHO AM I?

Tune: IDENTITY (JLB)

meditatively

Who am I? Not the one you choose. ___ Who

Em   C

am I? Not the one you lose. ___ Who am I? I'm the one from

Em   C   D   D7

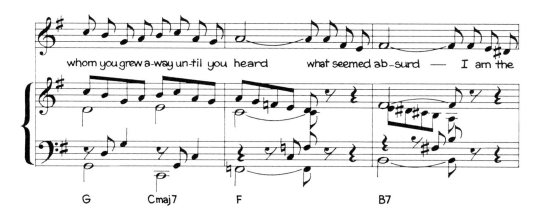

whom you grew a-way un-til you heard   what seemed ab-surd — I am the

G   Cmaj7   F   B7

1. Who am I?
   Not the one you choose.
   Who am I?
   Not the one you lose.
   Who am I? I'm the one
   From whom you grew away
   Until you heard what seemed absurd –
   I am the Way.

2. Who am I?
   I'm the one you tend
   In those whose lives
   Might break or mend.
   My hands, unknown, you've held,
   My people's pain you've quelled;
   Their gloom dispelled, you heard me say,
   "I am the Way."

3. Who am I?
   I'm the course of years,
   The force of life,
   The source of tears:
   The laughter in the room,
   The talking in the street
   Is where we meet. These too convey,
   I am the Way.

4. Who am I
   When regret or fear
   Demands you wonder
   Why you're here?
   I'm not the instant answer
   To your quick request.
   You should have read, I only said,
   "I am the Way."

5. Who are you?
   Not the one you were
   Before you learned
   To love and care.
   Who are you?
   You're the one
   With whom I want to share
   My faith, my food, my cross of wood,
   My will, my way.

This is essentially a solo song, well suited to be sung as slides, particularly of people doing a range of different things, are shown.

BLESSING AND HONOUR

Tune: BLESSING AND HONOUR (JLB)

brightly

BLESS—ING AND HON–OUR, WIS—DOM AND WEALTH, FREE–DOM TO SAVE OR TO

SE—VER: THESE WE PRO-CLAIM BE–LONG TO OUR GOD,

LORD OF CRE–A——TION FOR EV——ER.

Fine.

Harmony. Safe as the a—tom un—split in its shell, strong as the sea in in—

—ten — tion, fine as the weave of the dra—gon—fly's wing:

power is God's per — fect in—ven — tion.

(acc. only)

D.C.

Words and Music © 1987 The Iona Community

Chorus: BLESSING AND HONOUR, WISDOM AND WEALTH,
FREEDOM TO SAVE OR TO SEVER:
THESE WE PROCLAIM BELONG TO OUR GOD,
LORD OF CREATION FOR EVER.

1. Safe as the atom, unsplit in its shell,
    Strong as the sea in intention,
    Fine as the weave of the dragonfly's wing:
    Power is God's perfect invention.

2. Born of a woman and skilled at the lathe,
    Forfeiting glamour and glory,
    God, in the flesh of a carpenter's son,
    Practiced the power of a story.

3. Tempted to transform the stones into bread,
    Taunted to call help from heaven,
    Christ showed how strength lay in carrying the cross,
    Forgiving seventy times seven.

4. Power is made perfect where weakness is strong;
    Weakness is meant for our healing;
    Healing is found at the feet of the poor
    Where God, as servant, is kneeling.

5. Made in the image of one who, unarmed,
    Challenged the great and the greedy,
    Ours is the privilege to claim and express
    Justice for all who are needy.

If there is a choir or group who can sing the verses in harmony, and
keep the pitch, so much the better.

THE SUMMONS

Tune: KELVINGROVE (Scottish Trad.)

not too slowly

Will you come and fol—low me if I but call your name?___

(hum)

___ Will you go where you don't know and nev—er be the same?___

___ Will you let my love be shown, Will you let my name be known,

___ Will you let my life be grown in you and you in me?_____

Words and Arrangement © 1987 The Iona Community

1. Will you come and follow me
    If I but call your name?
    Will you go where you don't know
    And never be the same?
    Will you let my love be shown,
    Will you let my name be known,
    Will you let my life be grown
    In you and you in me?

2. Will you leave yourself behind
    If I but call your name?
    Will you care for cruel and kind
    And never be the same?
    Will you risk the hostile stare
    Should your life attract or scare?
    Will you let me answer prayer
    In you and you in me?

3. Will you let the blinded see
    If I but call your name?
    Will you set the prisoners free
    And never be the same?
    Will you kiss the leper clean,
    And do such as this unseen,
    And admit to what I mean
    In you and you in me?

4. Will you love the 'you' you hide
    If I but call your name?
    Will you quell the fear inside
    And never be the same?
    Will you use the faith you've found
    To reshape the world around,
    Through my sight and touch and sound
    In you and you in me?

5. Lord, your summons echoes true
    When you but call my name.
    Let me turn and follow you
    And never be the same.
    In your company I'll go
    Where your love and footsteps show.
    Thus I'll move and live and grow
    In you and you in me.

This song has been successfully used at commitment and confirmation services. Verse 4 is sung solo and those wishing to do so, leave their seats and move to the front of the congregation. Then all sing the last verse together. In some places, people may prefer to sing this song in 2/4 time, in which case simply change dotted minims to minims.

HERE AM I

Tune: TRAVELLER (JLB)

gently

In the warmth of the womb I met you, and I called you to life through the love of man and wife; In the warmth of the womb I met you say—ing, "Here am I."

1. In the warmth of the womb I met you,
   And I called you to life
   Through the love of man and wife;
   In the warmth of the womb I met you
   Saying, "Here am I".

2. As a baby in arms I met you,
   Wrapped in linen and care,
   Watched and welcomed everywhere;
   As a baby in arms I met you
   Saying, "Here am I".

3. In the tensions of youth I met you,
   Whether shy or uncouth,
   Always searching for the truth;
   In the tensions of youth I met you
   Saying, "Here am I".

4. In the quiet of your home I met you.
   When the door opened wide,
   Strangers came and out went pride;
   In the quiet of your home I met you
   Saying, "Here am I".

5. And wherever you go I will meet you,
   Till you draw your last breath
   In the birthplace known as death;
   Yes, wherever you go, I will meet you
   Saying, "Here am I".

Though not written for the purpose, this song may be effectively used at a baptism or confirmation.

JESUS IS LORD

Tune: MARBLE QUARRY (JLB)

with a stately rhythm

Je-sus is Lord of all, mon-arch of moun-tain and wave,

fus—er of wind and fire, sculp—tor of crag and cave.

Jes—us is Lord! God's might-y word cre—ates:

each feat—ure, worn or wild, to his in—tent re—lates.

Words and Music © 1987 The Iona Community

1. Jesus is Lord of all,
   Monarch of mountain and wave,
   Fuser of wind and fire,
   Sculptor of crag and cave.
   Jesus is Lord!
   God's mighty word creates:
   Each feature, worn or wild,
   To his intent relates.

2. Jesus is Prince of Peace:
   Atom and neutron must cower.
   Hate roots their suspect strength,
   But suffering love's his power.
   Jesus is Lord!
   God's mighty Word converts
   Weapons to welcome signs
   As foe to friend reverts.

3. Jesus is King of Love.
   Enemy, neighbour and friend;
   They, with the self, are bound
   In love which knows no end.
   Jesus is Lord!
   God's mighty Word engraves,
   Bold on the cross, that
   Christ-like love disturbs and saves.

4. Jesus is heaven's high priest;
   Earth is his altar below.
   Sectarian pride he chides
   That Christian faith may grow.
   Jesus is Lord!
   God's mighty Word unites.
   Those whom the past divides,
   He to the feast invites.

5. Jesus is Lord of Life!
   To him let every mind bend;
   For him let every pulse
   And nerve their purpose spend.
   Jesus is Lord!
   God's mighty Word requires
   Hands, heart and head
   To demonstrate what he inspires.

The tune is very expansive and should be sung, majestically, in unison.

THE STRANGEST OF SAINTS

Tune: WAE'S ME FOR PRINCE CHAIRLIE (Scottish Trad.)

brightly

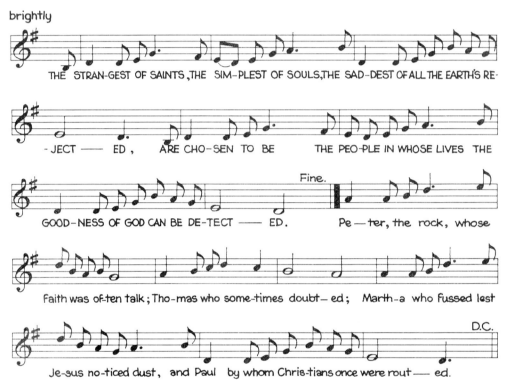

THE STRAN-GEST OF SAINTS, THE SIM-PLEST OF SOULS, THE SAD-DEST OF ALL THE EARTH'S RE-JECT — ED, ARE CHO-SEN TO BE THE PEO-PLE IN WHOSE LIVES THE GOOD-NESS OF GOD CAN BE DE-TECT — ED. Fine. Pe — ter, the rock, whose faith was of-ten talk; Tho-mas who some-times doubt— ed; Marth-a who fussed lest Je-sus no-ticed dust, and Paul by whom Chris-tians once were rout — ed. D.C.

122

Chorus: THE STRANGEST OF SAINTS,
THE SIMPLEST OF SOULS,
THE SADDEST OF ALL THE EARTH'S REJECTED,
ARE CHOSEN TO BE THE PEOPLE IN WHOSE LIVES
THE GOODNESS OF GOD CAN BE DETECTED.

1. Peter, the Rock, whose faith was often talk;
    Thomas who sometimes doubted;
    Martha who fussed, lest Jesus noticed dust,
    And Paul by whom Christians once were routed.

2. Names none can tell: a woman at the well,
    Widows and someone's mother;
    Men blind from birth, street children full of mirth,
    Ten lepers, each worse than every other.

3. Babes at the knee, a taxman in a tree;
    Women by men molested;
    Some who were bright and some who feared daylight,
    And many the privileged few detested.

4. Time can't diffuse the freshness of the news:
    Christ's friends are fully human;
    Failure and fear allow him to come near
    And understand every man and woman.

5. Who dare deride those found at Jesus' side,
    Welcome despite their weakness?
    Christ who knows all, expresses by his call
    The wonder of everyone's uniqueness.

With its wide range of characters, this song can be well illustrated by contemporary slides. An accompaniment for this song may be found on P. 54.

INSPIRED BY LOVE AND ANGER

Tune: SALLEY GARDENS (Irish Trad. arr. JLB)

gently

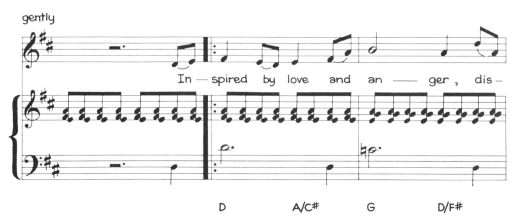

In — spired by love and an —— ger, dis-

D   A/C#   G   D/F#

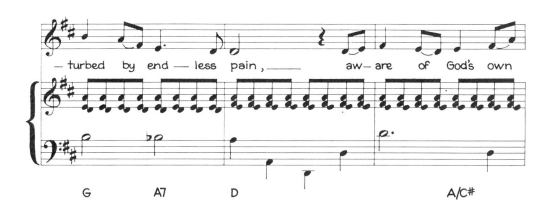

— turbed by end — less pain, —— aw — are of God's own

G   A7   D   A/C#

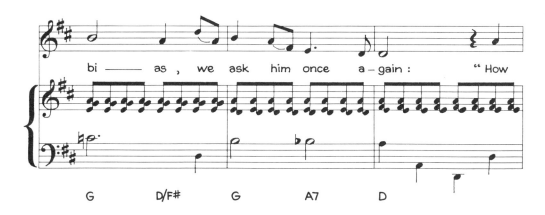

bi —— as, we ask him once a — gain : " How

G   D/F#   G   A7   D

1.   Inspired by love and anger, disturbed by need and pain,
     Informed of God's own bias, we ask him once again:
     "How long must some folk suffer? How long can few folk mind?
       How long dare vain self interest turn prayer and pity blind?"

2.   From those forever victims of heartless human greed,
     Their cruel plight composes a litany of need:
     "Where are the fruits of justice? Where are the signs of peace?
       When is the day when prisoners and dreams find their release?"

3.   From those forever shackled to what their wealth can buy,
     The fear of lost advantage provokes the bitter cry,
     "Don't query our position! Don't criticise our wealth!
       Don't mention those exploited by politics and stealth!"

4.   To God, who through the prophets proclaimed a different age,
     We offer earth's indifference, its agony and rage:
     "When will the wronged be righted? When will the kingdom come?
       When will the world be generous to all instead of some?"

5.   God asks, "Who will go for me? Who will extend my reach?
       And who, when few will listen, will prophecy and preach?
       And who, when few bid welcome, will offer all they know?
       And who, when few dare follow, will walk the road I show?"

6.   Amused in someone's kitchen, asleep in someone's boat,
     Attuned to what the ancients exposed, proclaimed and wrote,
     A saviour without safety, a tradesman without tools
     Has come to tip the balance with fishermen and fools.

Verses can be omitted to suit, though, given the beauty of the Irish
folk tune, the song may not feel long in singing it. As an alternative,
the *Passion Chorale* can be used with these words.

CHANTS AND RESPONSES

A SELECTION OF MEDITATIVE CHANTS AND RESPONSES

If we were to lose £1 for every person who screwed up their face when we first mention *chants*, and gain £1 for everyone who, afterwards, expressed their enjoyment, we would probably break even.

Chants and Responses have connotations of mumbo-jumbo language sung by marble-mouthed choirs. That may be true of the past, but today, thanks mainly to the work of the Taizé Community in France, many people are coming to enjoy using these in worship as a means whereby everyone can participate.

In much the same way as an evangelical *chorus*, a chant takes a line of prayer or scripture and allows it to be sung over and over again either to enable the worshipper to think more deeply about the significance of the words, or to relate the words to people or situations in need of prayer.

An example of the first use may be seen in the words,

KINDLE A FLAME TO LIGHTEN THE DARK
AND TAKE ALL FEAR AWAY.

Sitting in a darkened room, the chant may be begun. After a few singings, a candle is lit and put in the middle. People continue to sing and to offer to God everything in them which longs for light.

An example of the second use may be found with the chant,

LORD JESUS CHRIST, LOVER OF ALL,
TRAIL WIDE THE HEM OF YOUR GARMENT.
BRING HEALING, BRING PEACE.

If prayers are being offered for those who are ill or distressed, particularly at a service of healing, these words may be sung after a number of intercessions to gather up the intention of the whole congregation.

Sometime one chant may be used in both ways. Take, for example,

> I WAITED, I WAITED ON THE LORD.
> HE BENT DOWN LOW AND REMEMBERED ME
> WHEN HE HEARD MY PRAYER.

It may be that these words could be used for a personal recollection of God's goodness, or they may be used in between prayers for people who, in one way or another, are waiting for a change in their lives. Another example:

> DONA NOBIS PACEM IN TERRA,
> DONA NOBIS PACEM, DOMINE.
> (Give us peace on earth, O Lord)

These words could be used as part of a litany which mentions trouble spots in the world, or the chant may be sung as the bread and wine are passed at communion when we ask for Christ's peace in a very special way.

The last chant raises the issue of singing in a foreign language – Latin to be precise. Those who remember Vatican II will remember that Latin was knocked on the head then by the denomination which used it most. Why, then, continue to sing it?

There are two reasons. The first is that some things can be said far more neatly in Latin than in English and, once you know the words and are aware of their meaning, they then become vehicles for prayer. The second is that by occasionally using Latin we publicly express that we are part of the Holy Catholic Church which is a historical church. Using these words we stand beside those who worshipped God with them for over a thousand years. In musical matters, we do not stop singing *Adeste Fideles* to the words *O Come all ye faithful* just because it is an old tune. If either old words or old tunes can yet speak to the present age of Christians, there may be a case for retaining them. But, lest we thereby sanctify the past, we must always ask whether there is, in every instance, indeed a 'case'.

LIST OF CHANTS

WORDS	USE
COME, LORD, COME QUICKLY! COME, LORD, COME QUICKLY! COME, LORD JESUS, QUICKLY COME!	Sing during Advent or when- ever the worship requires that we say, 'Maranatha'.
DONA NOBIS PACEM IN TERRA, DONA NOBIS PACEM, DOMINE. (Give us peace on earth, O Lord.)	Peace and Justice events, Holy Communion. Close of Worship.
I WAITED, I WAITED ON THE LORD; I WAITED, I WAITED ON THE LORD; HE BENT DOWN LOW AND REMEMBERED ME WHEN HE HEARD MY PRAYER.	Prayers for those who are 'waiting'. Personal recollection. Advent.
JESUS CHRIST, SON OF GOD, HAVE MERCY UPON US.	Prayers of confession. Holy Communion.
KINDLE A FLAME TO LIGHTEN THE DARK AND TAKE ALL FEAR AWAY.	Group or personal meditation. Sing while candles are being lit before or during worship.
LORD, DRAW NEAR. LORD, DRAW NEAR. DRAW NEAR, DRAW NEAR AND STAY.	Beginning of worship. Prayers for lonely people. General intercessions.
LORD JESUS CHRIST, LOVER OF ALL, TRAIL WIDE THE HEM OF YOUR GARMENT. BRING HEALING, BRING PEACE.	Prayers for the sick. Services of healing.
LORD, TO WHOM SHALL WE GO? YOURS ARE THE WORDS OF ETERNAL LIFE.	Sing as a response after say- ings of Jesus.
MAGNIFICAT ANIMA MEA DOMINUM. (My soul praises the Lord).	Advent and Christmas, espe- cially in relation to Mary's experience.
THROUGH OUR LIVES AND BY OUR PRAYERS, YOUR KINGDOM COME.	General intercessions.
VENI IMMANUEL (O Come, Emmanuel)	Advent.
WITH GOD, ALL THINGS ARE POSSIBLE; ALL THINGS ARE POSSIBLE WITH GOD.	After promises of Jesus. General intercessions.

COME, LORD, COME QUICKLY

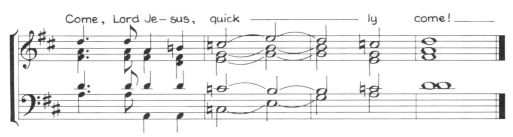

DONA NOBIS PACEM IN TERRA

I WAITED ON THE LORD

Music © 1987 The Iona Community

JESUS CHRIST, SON OF GOD

Music © 1987 The Iona Community

KINDLE A FLAME TO LIGHTEN THE DARK

Music © 1987 The Iona Community

LORD, DRAW NEAR

Music © 1987 The Iona Community

LORD JESUS CHRIST, LOVER OF ALL

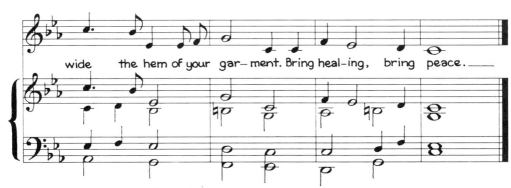

LORD, TO WHOM SHALL WE GO?

MAGNIFICAT

THROUGH OUR LIVES AND BY OUR PRAYERS

VENI IMMANUEL

WITH GOD ALL THINGS ARE POSSIBLE

TEN GOLDEN RULES

for enabling the least confident of people
to teach new songs
to the most cynical of congregations.

1. Believe in the voice which God has given you.
   It is the voice of an apprentice angel.

2. Believe in the voices God has given other people.

   Years of being told, and telling themselves, that they cannot sing can be redeemed by the confidence you show in other's abilities.

3. Teach only songs or harmony lines which you personally have sung in your bath or your bed.

   If you are uncertain about a song, that will be the first thing your 'trainees' detect.

4. Teach songs only at the appropriate time . . . . which is seldom if ever during a church service or even after the organ voluntary.

   The best time to teach is before anything happens, while people are still settling down. If they learn a new song then, they will recognise it as a familiar friend when used later in the service. **Never** antagonise a congregation by teaching a new song the minute before it is to be used.

5. Always introduce a new song with enthusiasm; never with an apology.

   To tell a group of people that they 'have' to learn a new song and that they 'might' pick it up is as appropriate as a tickling stick at a funeral.

6. Use only your voice and hands to teach new tunes.

   Human beings find it easier to imitate another human being than to copy a 12 string guitar, grand piano or pipe organ. They also pick up the pitch and rhythm of notes when thay are signed in the air much more easily than when they are merely sung.

7. When teaching, sing a bit worse than your best and always use your normal voice.

   Remember, you are asking people to copy another person, not to be amused or threatened by the vocal dexterity of a real or would-be operatic superstar.

8. Let the people know about the structure of a tune before you teach it, then teach it in recognisable sections.

> e.g. if the 1st, 2nd & 4th lines are the same (as happens in many folk tunes), tell people that. Then you only have to teach two lines – the first (which is repeated later) and the second;
>
> if the tune has a chorus, tell people that. Then teach them the chorus, and once they have it, you sing the verses while they sing the chorus, gradually picking up the verse tune en route.
>
> **but**
>
> if the tune does go fairly high, don't petrify people in advance by making a pained expression before the top note. Teach it down a key and later raise the pitch when people are familiar with it.

9. When demonstrating:

   a) sing a verse or a verse & chorus over first

   b) teach a breath or two lines at a time, whichever is shortest

   c) don't teach a new phrase until the present one is recognisable

   d) sing the tune to 'la' if it looks too big a job to get words and music together at the first go

   e) after the song has been taught, you sing a verse through once, asking people to listen to you and correct, inwardly, their potential mistakes, if any

   f) ask everyone to sing the same verse together (if long verses) or the next verse (if short verses)

   g) always thank and encourage those who are learning.

10. When using the song, already learned, in worship, try not to have all the people singing all the time.

Either get a soloist to do verse 1, thus refreshing everyone's memory; or get a small group or soloist to sing most of the verses and others join in the chorus, if there is one; or alternate verses between men and women, sides of the church or whatever. People enjoy a song much more when they don't have to sing all of it.

To get the right pitch, use a pitch pipe, chime bar or recorder.

To get people started, you sing the first line to 'la'. To get people singing well, you sit among them and if 'they' are expected to help lead the congregation to sing, think about positioning them not in the front of everyone, but behind or among other people.

To get the best from new songs, do not teach too many at one time.

WILD GOOSE SONGS – Volume 1

Alphabetical Index of First Lines

COPYRIGHT

OTHER PUBLICATIONS

The Iona Community has an increasing range of worship and resource materials, tapes etc., which may be purchased on a retail basis or wholesale. For a catalogue and further details, apply to Wild Goose Resources Group at the above address.

CURRENT PUBLICATIONS OF THE IONA COMMUNITY

THE WHOLE EARTH SHALL CRY GLORY	Paperback	ISBN 0 947988 00 9
THE WHOLE EARTH SHALL CRY GLORY	Hardback	ISBN 0 947900 04 1
Iona prayers by Rev. George F. MacLeod		
THE IONA COMMUNITY WORSHIP BOOK		ISBN 0 947988 28 9
Iona Community		
THE CORACLE – REBUILDING THE COMMON LIFE		ISBN 0 947988 25 4
Jubilee reprint of Foundation Documents of the Iona Community		
PEACE AND ADVENTURE		ISBN 0 95013516 X
Ellen Murray		
90 RECIPES FROM THE IONA COMMUNITY		ISBN 0 947988 17 3
Sue Pattison		
RE-INVENTING THEOLOGY		ISBN 0 947988 29 7
Ian M. Fraser		
MEANING THE LORD'S PRAYER		ISBN 0 947988 30 0
George T. H. Reid		
PARABLES AND PATTER		ISBN 0 947988 33 5
Erik Cramb		
WILD GOOSE SONGS – VOLUME 1		ISBN 0 947988 23 8
John Bell & Graham Maule		
WILD GOOSE SONGS – VOLUME 2		ISBN 0 947988 27 0
John Bell & Graham Maule		
LOVE FROM BELOW (Wild Goose Songs Volume 3)		ISBN 0 947988 34 3
John Bell & Graham Maule		
A TOUCHING PLACE	Cassette	No.IC/WGP/004
Wild Goose Worship Group		
CLOTH FOR THE CRADLE	Cassette	No.IC/WGP/007
Wild Goose Worship Group		
LOVE FROM BELOW	Cassette	No.IC/WGP/008
Wild Goose Worship Group		
FOLLY AND LOVE	Cassette	No.IC/WGP/005
Iona Abbey		
FREEDOM IS COMING	Cassette	No.IC/WGP/006
FREEDOM IS COMING		ISBN 91 86788 15 7
Utryck		
THROUGH WOOD AND NAILS	Record	No.146/REC/S
Iona Abbey		
WILD GOOSE PRINTS No.1		ISBN 0 947988 06 8
John Bell & Graham Maule		
WILD GOOSE PRINTS No.2		ISBN 0 947988 10 6
John Bell & Graham Maule		
WILD GOOSE PRINTS No.3		ISBN 0 947988 24 6
John Bell & Graham Maule		
WILD GOOSE PRINTS No.4		ISBN 0 947988 35 1
John Bell & Graham Maule		
EH ... JESUS ... YES, PETER ...? Book 1		ISBN 0 947988 20 3
John Bell & Graham Maule		
EH ... JESUS ... YES, PETER ...? Book 2		ISBN 0 947988 31 9
John Bell & Graham Maule		
WHAT IS THE IONA COMMUNITY?		ISBN 0 947988 07 6
Iona Community		
CO-OPERATION VERSUS EXPLOITATION		ISBN 0 947988 22 X
Walter Fyfe		
COLUMBA		ISBN 0 947988 11 4
Mitchell Bunting		
FEEL IT – Detached Youth Work In Action		ISBN 0 947988 32 7
Cilla McKenna		
PRAISING A MYSTERY		Hope Ref. 749
Brian Wren		
BRING MANY NAMES		747
Brian Wren		

Wild Goose Publications